UNIVERSITY SPACE PLANNING

UNIVERSITY OF ILLINOIS PRESS   URBANA · CHICAGO · LONDON 1968

UNIVERSITY SPACE PLANNING

**TRANSLATING
THE EDUCATIONAL PROGRAM
OF A UNIVERSITY
INTO PHYSICAL FACILITY REQUIREMENTS**

by HARLAN D. BAREITHER
and JERRY L. SCHILLINGER

© 1968 by the Board of Trustees of the University of Illinois
Manufactured in the United States of America
Library of Congress Catalog Card No. 68-22271

252 78404 9

FOREWORD

In the administrative vocabulary of universities, the word "space" perhaps more than any other symbolizes the internal pressures and external constraints that shape the growth of a comprehensive institution of higher education. Demand for more and better space arises from many conditions: long-standing shortages, faster obsolescence of facilities, increasing complexity of programs (especially in the sciences), inordinate expansion of enrollment, new instructional programs, and society's rising expectation of direct help from universities in solving its problems. The struggle to satisfy all of these needs becomes increasingly difficult in the face of escalating construction costs, competing internal demands for operating funds, and the insistent claims upon the nation's resources originating outside higher education.

It is understandable, therefore, that many universities have been moving rapidly to develop more systematic administrative techniques for the analysis and evaluation of institutional operations — looking toward improved utilization of existing resources and more effective "planning, programming, and budgeting" for the future. The present volume reflects a significant effort in this direction which began ten years ago at the University of Illinois when Professor Harlan D. Bareither of the Department of Mechanical and Industrial Engineering was appointed Director of a Central Office on the Use of Space, reporting to the Vice-President and Provost.

Initially, the main function of the new office was the control and assignment of classrooms, and Director Bareither continued to devote a substantial part of his time to teaching. Even this limited degree of "central control" of the use of space was not received with widespread acclaim by departments which long had enjoyed a kind of de facto jurisdiction over conveniently located classrooms. The benefits of orderly scheduling, however, soon became so evident that opposition quickly declined to a normal level for a well-administered regulation affecting faculty members.

The responsibilities of the Director of the Central Office on the Use of Space expanded over the years to include a wide range of both "line" and "staff" functions — the former limited to the Urbana-Champaign campus and the latter being university-wide in nature (reflecting the dual role of the Executive

Vice-President and Provost until a chancellorship was established at the Urbana-Champaign campus in July, 1967). The Director's "line" responsibilities at the Urbana-Champaign campus have consisted mainly of these activities: (a) maintenance of an inventory of all physical facilities, systematically classified and encoded for computer processing; (b) recommendation of assignments and reassignments of all nonresidential space; (c) scheduling the use of classrooms, auditoriums, and other nondepartmental space; and (d) preparation of the official timetable of course offerings each term. The "staff" responsibilities have been university-wide in nature, and are mainly the following: (a) the development and recommendation of utilization standards for all types of nonresidential space; (b) coordination of the preparation of program statements specifying the kinds and amounts of space to be included in new buildings; (c) coordinating the preparation of requests submitted to federal agencies for grants under the Higher Education Facilities Act; (d) serving as a staff officer to the University Building Program Committee; and (e) acting as the university's liaison representative in space matters to the Illinois Board of Higher Education and other outside agencies.

It would perhaps be useful to record the latest stage in the organization of these varied space functions at the University of Illinois both as additional background for the present volume and because the information might be of interest to other multicampus universities. The essential changes in space administration with the establishment of the chancellorship system have been the creation of these offices: (a) an Office of Space Utilization at each of the university's three campuses, whose director reports to the Chancellor (or a designated associate) and performs the "line" responsibilities outlined above, as well as certain local staff functions; (b) a University Office of Space Programming under the direction of Professor Bareither, who still reports to the Executive Vice-President and Provost, with some expansion of the staff responsibilities noted above.

The present volume is an account of the principal technical achievements of the former Central Office on the Use of Space during the decade of evolution of the administrative structure and functions just described. In essence, what Messrs. Bareither and Schillinger present in this volume is a systematic methodology for deriving the space requirements of a university — given analytical specifications of its educational program. Although obviously relying upon assumptions and judgments in such matters as student-teacher ratio and laboratory area per scientist, their procedure has the great merit of requiring explicit identification of such underlying standards. This makes it relatively easy to "cross-validate" them by comparisons with those for similar departments within or outside the university.

One of the interesting aspects of the development and application of the "Numeric Method," as it is called, has been the relatively widespread acceptance of the approach by department heads and faculty members. Although they sometimes have had highly exaggerated ideas about the amount of space needed for a department or a laboratory, after going through the analytical process prescribed herein they usually have found the results acceptable. This has probably been due partly to the pragmatic approach followed in arriving at standards for space in which individual faculty members have unique interests, such as research laboratories. This has typically involved detailed discussion of the equipment and activities to be housed, comparisons with similar facilities here or elsewhere, and finally agreement on acceptable space requirements.

Concerning the specific values that appear, the authors stress that they should not be regarded as fixed standards. This point should be strongly re-emphasized. The underlying assumptions as to the size of staff required for a given educational program, for example, are subject to continuing review; and staff size obviously is an important determinant of space requirements. Revisions of specific figures are to be expected, therefore, as the process of internal checking and cross-validation against practices elsewhere are pursued. The permanent value of this work — as the authors also stress — lies mainly in its analytical methodology. The systematic cultivation of the conceptual framework and the procedures described in this volume should lead to more equitable assignment of an institution's existing space, to more efficient programming of its future space requirements, and hence to substantial economics in both capital and operating costs.

Lyle H. Lanier
Executive Vice-President and Provost
University of Illinois

ACKNOWLEDGMENTS

        The material in this book has been derived from the activities of the authors in the performance of their duties at the Central Office on the Use of Space at the University of Illinois. In addition, many ideas have been obtained from conversations and exchange of data with James Blakesley, Administrative Coordinator of Schedules and Space at Purdue University; Harold Dahnke, Director of Space Utilization at Michigan State University; William Fuller, Director of Higher Education Facilities Planning, State of New York; Frederick E. Schwehr, Associate Director, Coordinating Council for Higher Education, State of Wisconsin; and Donovan E. Smith, Specialist of Physical Planning, University of California.

  In any subject as complex as facilities planning involving a number of people, there will be disagreements as to methodology and procedures. Because of this possibility the authors assume complete responsibility for the content and points of view reflected in this book.

CONTENTS

1. Introduction 1

2. Description of the Planning Process and Definition of Terms 3

3. Inventory of Physical Facilities 19

4. Institutional Data 41

5. Projection of Physical Facilities by the "Numeric Method" 51

6. The "Numeric Method" Applied to the Educational Programs in Law and Veterinary Medicine 71

7. Summarization and Presentation of Physical Facility Data 82

8. Planning of Specific Capital Outlay Projects 91

Appendix A 97

Appendix B 100

Appendix C 122

Appendix D 125

Appendix E 149

Index 151

INTRODUCTION

Millions of federal, state, and local dollars are being spent annually by colleges and universities throughout the United States for new physical facilities. A large number of inquiries by other colleges and universities regarding planning methods and procedures indicate that many such institutions of higher learning have not made appraisals of their existing physical facilities, nor have they developed planning and projection methods to program the type of facilities required. As a result of an increasing number of inquiries from colleges, universities, and architectural firms, the authors have assembled and presented under one cover a philosophy, method, and procedure for the analysis of physical facility requirements for institutions of higher education as used at the University of Illinois. Therefore, this book will address itself to the complex problem of translating the educational program of a university into physical facility requirements. It will set forth the basic procedure by which the existing and future facilities of an institution of higher education can be defined, analyzed, and projected in a systematic manner to coincide with the educational goals set forth by its governing agency.

A procedure called the "Numeric Method" has been developed which will provide the framework for translating the educational program into physical facility requirements. The methodology presented provides satisfactory answers to the following basic questions which should be answered for any method of projecting and analyzing physical facilities.

1. What types of physical facilities are required for the educational program?
2. What will generate the requirements?
3. Will the system used to generate the physical facilities treat all fields of study objectively?
4. Is the system designed to permit comparison of data with other universities?

The general philosophy of the "Numeric Method" for determining requirements is that the physical facility requirements may be categorized into what will be called "building blocks." For each "building block," there exists an index which will generate the space requirements. The total amount of space required at an institution for each "building block" is dependent upon the number of FTE (full-time equivalent) students, the level of student, the fields of study, the institutional philosophy pertaining to scheduling patterns, size of library, etc.

The "Numeric Method" for projecting space requirements has been developed so that it can be applied to all sizes and types of institutions of higher learning. Institutions, like people, have different characteristics. In many cases, standards have been recommended which have been applicable to the University of Illinois. The actual value of the proposed standard may not be adaptable to every institution due to differences in philosophies; however, if a different standard value is used, the logic and procedure can still be applied. In addition to being an internal management tool for allocating existing facilities and for determining future physical facilities required, this system was developed to serve as a basis for evaluating capital budgets by boards of higher education or legislative groups.

Flexibility is the main feature of the "Numeric Method" in that utilization rates other than those recommended can be used and still provide a valid and useful system for analysis. Thus it is possible to use the "Numeric Method" for a process of decision making at the administrative level of an institution by making calculations based on various methods of offering the educational programs and determining the space requirements based upon constant utilization rates or varying the utilization rates.

The data presented here pertaining to the "Numeric Method" does not apply to the health sciences such as the schools of medicine, dentistry, nursing, and pharmacy. It is hoped that in the future these areas of study can be analyzed and projected in the same manner as presented in this book; however, it is anticipated that many months of study will be necessary before this task can be accomplished. Also, it should be noted that considerable studies on greenhouse space and farm buildings have indicated that the requirements are more closely tied to the specific types of experimentations than to the number of faculty or students. Therefore, these two types of space will not be analyzed in this book. No attempt will be made to elaborate on the mechanics of adapting the systems and procedures presented here to electronic data-processing equipment because such a discussion should be considered a separate topic and because data-processing equipment available varies quite markedly from one university to another.

The data presented here deal only with the translation of the educational program into physical facilities for a university; it is recognized that the total institutional planning involves consideration of traffic flow (pedestrian and vehicle), vehicle parking, utility requirements, and land acquisition. However, it is felt that the educational program must be defined and, in turn, the physical facility requirements be determined before the overall university planning can begin.

DESCRIPTION OF THE PLANNING PROCESS AND DEFINITION OF TERMS

The translation of the educational program into physical facility requirements involves a constant evaluation and re-evaluation of the enrollment projections, changes in educational program, inventory of existing facilities, and the development of new facilities dependent upon departmental requirements.

This process involves many segments of the university. The manner in which a university organizes to accomplish translating the educational program into physical facility requirements is a matter of institutional preference. However, regardless of the organization, certain jobs need to be done, and it is the purpose of this chapter to give an overview of the total planning process and then to acquaint the reader with the most common terms and definitions used in analyzing and projecting physical facility requirements.

The steps to be followed are shown in Figure 1 and are presented in the sequence in which they should be undertaken. Although the figure presents the steps required for a complete analysis, it should be recognized that each step must be constantly reviewed to reflect the dynamic changes that are taking place in institutions of higher learning.

Step 1 *Learn the Language.* Before beginning any study of physical facility requirements, it is necessary to become familiar with the terms and definitions used in the field.

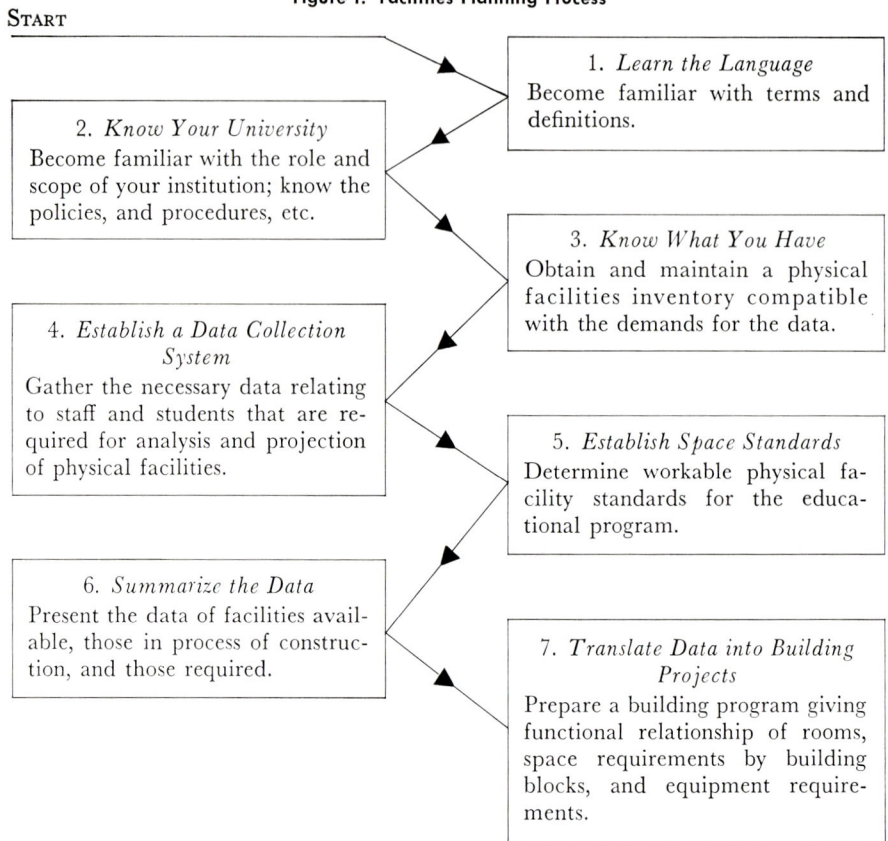

Figure 1. Facilities Planning Process

Step 2 *Know Your University.* An understanding of the university's educational goals, its policies, and its procedures is a most important step in the planning process. A review and understanding of the goals of an institution will provide the necessary insight into its past and future policies and procedures. This is necessary because educational goals and programs can vary widely among institutions of higher learning. A familiarization with the policies and procedures of the institution will prove very valuable in the analysis and projection of physical facilities because it will involve the coordination and cooperation of many individuals. Space planning within the university cannot be effective unless there is understanding, cooperation, and interaction among all concerned.

Step 3 *Know What You Have.* Before any assessment of future needs can be made, a thorough knowledge of the existing physical facilities must be acquired. It is essential that the data obtained are compatible with that which will be used later for projection of facilities. Chapter 3 presents some methods and procedures for establishing and maintaining an inventory of the existing physical facilities.

Step 4 *Establish a Data Collection System.* The gathering of the proper institutional data for space analysis and projection is one of the most difficult tasks in the planning process. In general, it involves the coordination of several units on the campus. As the institution becomes more involved in graduate work, assembling the institutional data becomes more complex. Chapter 4 indentifies and discusses the specific institutional data required for the analysis and projection of physical facilities.

Step 5 *Establish Space Standards*. The establishment and adoption of workable physical facility standards that will treat all areas of study objectively is the goal. To accomplish this goal, a system called the "Numeric Method" has been developed and is presented in Chapters 5 and 6.

Step 6 *Summarize the Data*. Once the institutional data and standards have been obtained, the actual calculation of the space required per academic unit is a relatively simple task. These data are then summarized and presented to various levels of the administration for review and determination of new construction required. Chapter 7 presents suggested formats for summarization of inventory of existing facilities, space previously approved for construction, space to be razed, and space required as a result of projected enrollments.

Step 7 *Translate the Calculations Into a Building Program*. After the reviews of Step 6 have been accomplished, a determination of departments or units that need additional space can be made. The next step is to decide upon the building which should be constructed to effectively meet these needs. Chapter 8 identifies and defines the steps, procedures, and methods involved in planning a specific building.

The implementation of the planning process will require standardization of terms and will involve many of the existing offices of the university. This usually results in fears of loss of authority, identity, control, and voice in university affairs. The offices involved will be reticent to accept any new procedures unless the "administration" is in accord with a standardized process of planning and becomes actively involved in its development. Lines of communication must be established with the educational units to inform them of the benefits of the types of data that may be supplied to them as aids to the planning of future facilities. The planning staff must make a continuous effort to coordinate the flow of data to all the educational units to secure their cooperation.

These educational units must be informed of the meanings of the most common terms and definitions used in projecting physical facility requirements. The following list of definitions is in no manner meant to be complete; if the reader desires a more complete set of definitions, the following sources are available:

Handbook of Data and Definitions in Higher Education. A service of the Joint Committee on Data and Definitions in Higher Education Sponsored by the Association of Collegiate Registrars and Admissions Officers (A.A.C.R.A.O., 1962).

Manual for Studies of Space Utilization in Colleges and Universities, by John Dale Russell and James Doi (American Association of Collegiate Registrars and Admissions Officers, 1957).

TERMS USED IN THE MEASUREMENT OF PHYSICAL FACILITIES

1. Gross Area

The gross area of a building has been defined by the U.S. Department of Health, Education, and Welfare; the National Association of Physical Plant Administrators; the American Standards Association; the American Institute of Architects; and the National Academy of Sciences — National Research Council. These definitions are essentially the same. The major differences are the manner in which unenclosed roofed-over areas are evaluated. The two definitions of gross area most widely used by institutions of higher learning are those given by the American Institute of Architects and the National Academy of Sciences — National Research Council. Because of their extensive use, both definitions are given below:

The American Institute of Architects AIA Doc. D101
September 1963 Edition — Page 1
ARCHITECTURAL AREA OF BUILDINGS

The ARCHITECTURAL AREA of a building is the sum of the areas of the several floors of the building, including basements, mezzanine and intermediate floored tiers and penthouses of headroom height, measured from the exterior faces of exterior walls or from the center line of walls separating buildings.

Covered walkways, open roofed-over areas that are paved, porches and similar spaces shall have the architectural area multiplied by an area factor of 0.50.

The architectural area does not include such features as pipe trenches, exterior terraces or steps, chimneys, roof overhangs, etc.

Classification of Building Areas
Technical Report No. 50 for the Federal Construction Council
by Task Group T-56, Publication 1235
National Academy of Sciences — National Research Council,
Washington, D.C., 1964

Gross Area

a. Definition

"Gross Area" should be construed to mean the sum of the floor areas included within the outside faces of exterior walls for all stories, or areas, which have floor surfaces.

b. Basis for Measurement

Gross area should be computed by measuring from the outside face of exterior walls, disregarding cornices, pilasters, buttresses, etc., which extend beyond the wall face.

c. Description

In addition to ground to top-story internal floored spaces obviously covered in "a" above, gross area should include basements (except unexcavated portions), attics, garages, enclosed porches, penthouses and mechanical equipment floors, lobbies, mezzanines, all balconies — inside or outside — utilized for operational functions, and corridors, provided they are within the outside face lines of the building. Roofed loading or shipping platforms should be included whether within or outside the exterior face lines of the building.

d. Limitations

Open courts and light wells, or portions of upper floors eliminated by rooms or lobbies which rise above single-floor ceiling height, should not be included in the gross area, nor should unenclosed roofed-over areas or floored surfaces with less than 6 feet 6 inches clear head-room be included unless they can properly be designated and used as either net assignable, mechanical, circulation, or custodial area.

The definition proposed in the report *Classification of Building Areas* is a result of a study conducted by a task group of specialists from nine federal government agencies and was published in 1964. Because of the recent issue of this report and probability that this definition will be used by all federal agencies and the majority of institutions in the future, it will be used throughout this book.

2. Net Assignable Area

There does not appear to be a great difference in this definition among the various organizations. The main differences found in the definition of net assignable area are in the terminology. Some schools use the term "net area" when they mean the same thing as "net assignable area." Other schools use "assignable area" when they mean the same thing as "net assignable area." To prevent any misconception of the term, the terminology "net assignable area" is used.

"Net assignable area," or net assignable square feet (NASF) as used in this text, is probably the most important area to be considered by the space analysts, as it is the amount of area which can be used by the occupants of the building. Because of the slight differences, the only definition of "net assignable area" given in this book is that proposed in *Classification of Building Areas*.

a. Definition

"Net Assignable Area" should be construed to mean the sum of all areas on all floors of a building assigned to, or available for assignment to, an occupant, including every type of space functionally usable by an occupant (excepting those spaces elsewhere separately defined — see 3, 4, and 5 below).

b. Basis for Measurement

All areas comprising the net assignable should be computed by measuring from the inside finish of permanent outer building walls, to the office side of corridors and/or to permanent partitions. (Some buildings are constructed to have two corridors on a floor, thus providing interior rooms. Under these conditions, the net assignable space of the rooms will be obtained by measuring from the inside surfaces of the enclosing walls.)

c. Description

Included should be space subdivisions for offices, file rooms, office storage rooms, etc., including those for special purposes (e.g., auditoriums, cafeterias, courtrooms, telephone and telegraph rooms, garages), which can be put to useful purposes in accomplishment of an agency mission.

d. Limitations

Deductions should not be made for columns and projections necessary to the building.

3. Custodial Area

The definition of custodial area differs little among the various agencies, and only that presented in *Classification of Building Areas* will be given in this manual.

a. Definition

"Custodial Area" should be construed to mean the sum of all areas on all floors of a building used for building protection, care, maintenance, and operation.

b. Basis for Measurement

These areas should be measured from the inside surfaces of enclosing walls.

c. Description
Included should be such areas as guardrooms, shops, locker rooms, janitors' closets, maintenance storerooms.

d. Limitations
Deductions should not be made for columns and projections necessary to the building.

4. Circulation Area

The definition given below is that proposed in *Classification of Building Areas*.

a. Definition
"Circulation Area" should be construed to mean that portion of the gross area — whether or not enclosed by partitions — which is required for physical access to some subdivision of space.

b. Basis for Measurement
Circulation area should be computed by measuring from the inner faces of the walls or partitions which enclose horizontal spaces used for such purposes; or, when such spaces are not enclosed by walls or partitions, measurements should be taken from imaginary lines which conform as nearly as possible to the established circulation pattern of the building.

c. Description
Circulation area should include, but not be limited to: corridors (access, public, service, also "phantom": for large unpartitioned areas); elevator shafts; escalators; fire towers or stairs; stairs and stair halls; loading platforms (except when required for operational reasons and, thus, includable in net assignable area); lobbies (elevator, entrance, public; also, public vestibules); tunnels and bridges (not mechanical).

d. Limitations
When assuming corridor areas, only horizontal spaces required for general access should be included — not aisles which are normally used only for circulation within offices or other working areas. Deductions should not be made for columns and projections necessary to the building.

5. Mechanical Area

The definition given is that proposed in *Classification of Building Areas*. There may be some slight difference between this definition and that given by other agencies. Some agencies group the nonprivate toilet facilities, circulation areas, and custodial areas in the category of public service area. Thus, the definition used must be checked before any comparisons are made.

a. Definition
"Mechanical Area" should be construed to mean that portion of the gross area designed to house mechanical equipment, utility services and non-private toilet facilities.

b. Basis for Measurement
Mechanical area should be computed by measuring from the inner faces of the walls, partitions, or screens which enclose such areas.

c. Description
Mechanical area should include, but not be limited to: air-duct shafts; boiler rooms; fixed mechanical and electrical equipment rooms; fuel rooms; mechanical service shafts; meter and communications closets; service chutes; stacks; and non-private toilet rooms (custodial and public).

d. Limitations
Deductions should not be made for columns and projections necessary to the building.

6. Construction Area

The definition given is that proposed in *Classification of Building Areas*. In essence, the construction is that area remaining after items 2, 3, 4, and 5 have been subtracted from gross area.

a. Definition

"Construction Area" should be construed to mean that portion of the gross area which cannot be put to use because of the presence of structural features of the building.

b. Basis for Measurement

Precise computation of construction area is not contemplated under these definitions — some construction features are included in the computation of other areas. However, total construction area should generally be determined by assuming it to be the residual area after the net assignable, circulation, custodial, and mechanical areas have been subtracted from the gross area.

c. Description

Examples of areas normally classified as construction area are exterior walls, fire walls, permanent partitions and unusable areas in attics, basements, or comparable portions of the building.

7. Interior Area

This term, although not included in *Classification of Building Areas*, is used by some agencies and offices in analyzing the area used for exterior walls and other exterior projections on buildings.

a. Definition

"Interior Space Area" of a building means the total area measured between the principal exterior wall faces of the building. (Some agencies use interior space area of a building to mean the total area between the principal wall faces, at or near floor level, plus wallcase or alcove spaces, or both, opening into and designed to serve the activity carried on in that area. When this definition is applied to a building, it will result in the summation of the net assignable area, the custodial area, the circulation area and the mechanical area.)

An example of the application of the various areas to a simple floor plan of a two-story building with a penthouse for mechanical equipment follows.

Figure 2. Building Elevations

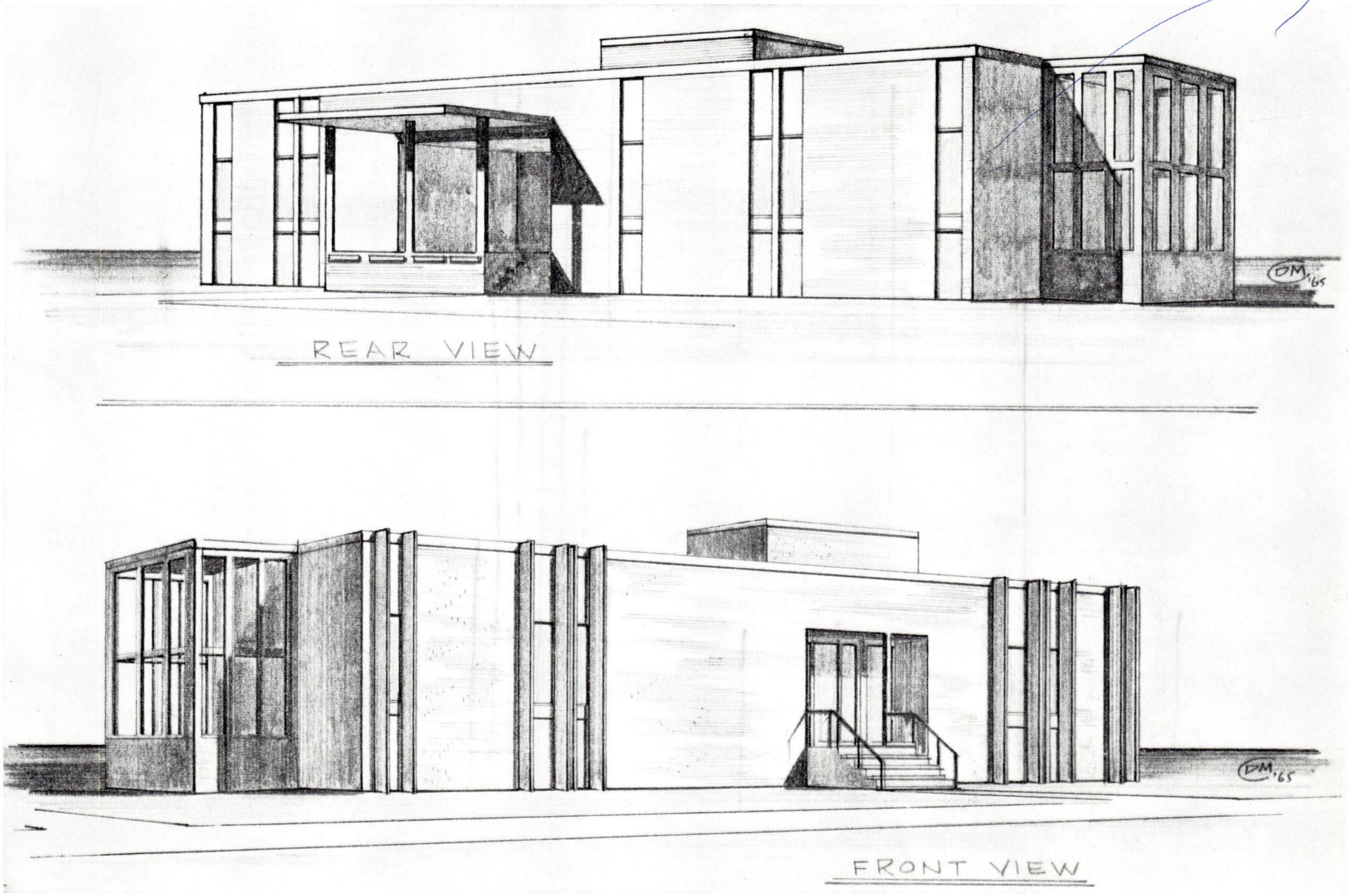

DESCRIPTION OF THE PLANNING PROCESS AND DEFINITION OF TERMS 11

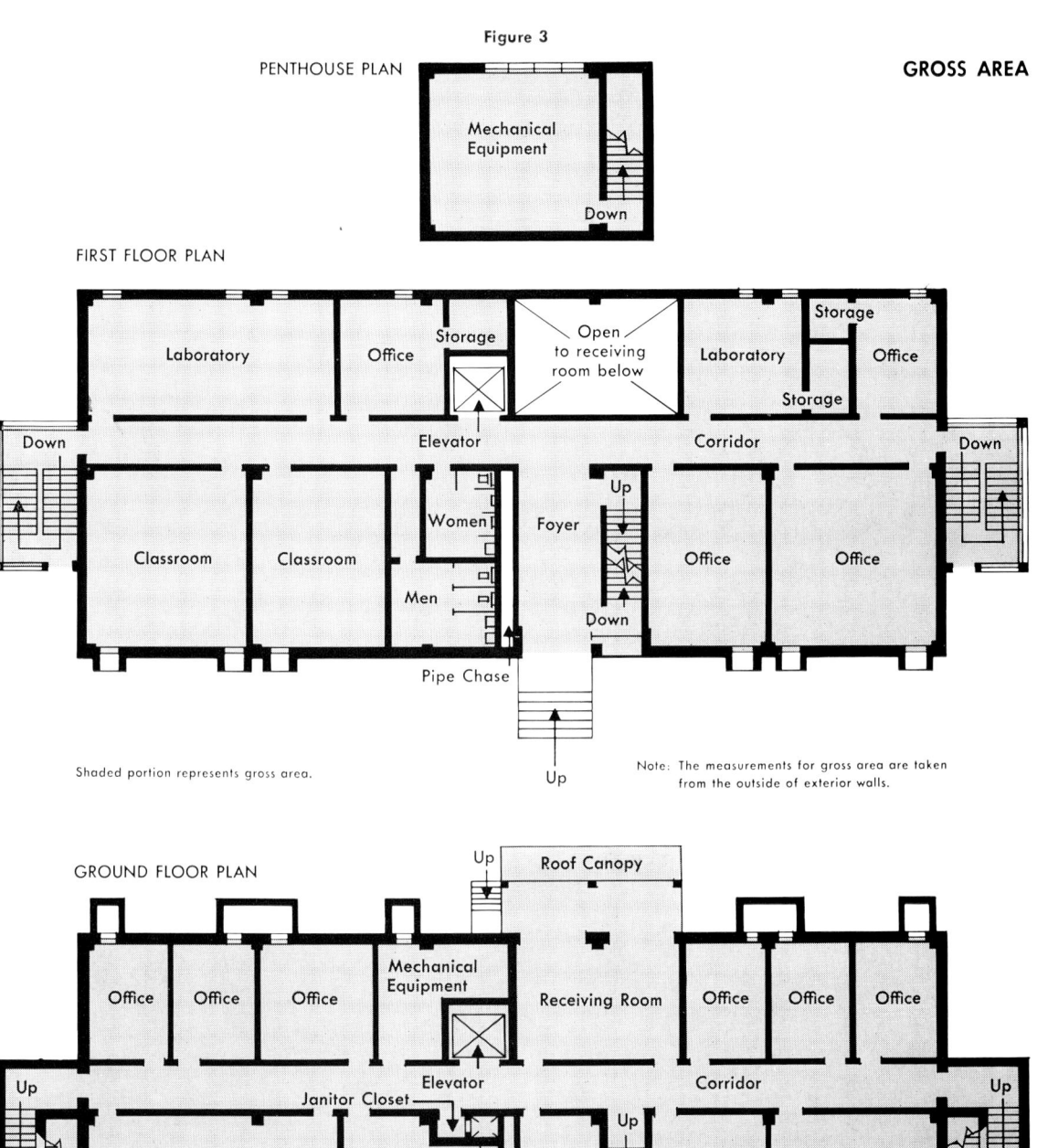

Figure 3

PENTHOUSE PLAN

GROSS AREA

FIRST FLOOR PLAN

Shaded portion represents gross area.

Note: The measurements for gross area are taken from the outside of exterior walls.

GROUND FLOOR PLAN

12 UNIVERSITY SPACE PLANNING

Figure 4

NET ASSIGNABLE SQUARE FEET

PENTHOUSE PLAN

FIRST FLOOR PLAN

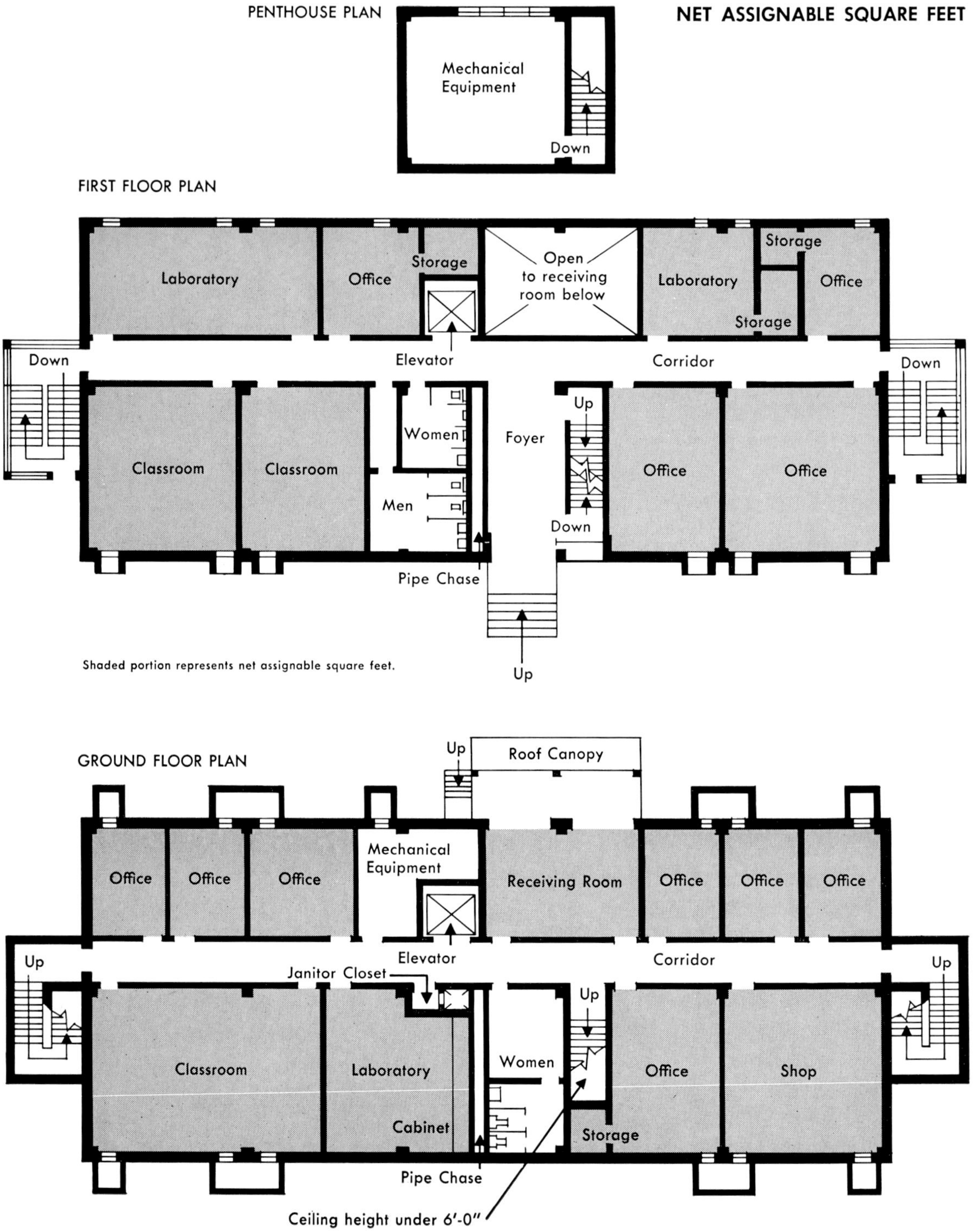

Shaded portion represents net assignable square feet.

GROUND FLOOR PLAN

Ceiling height under 6'-0"

DESCRIPTION OF THE PLANNING PROCESS AND DEFINITION OF TERMS 13

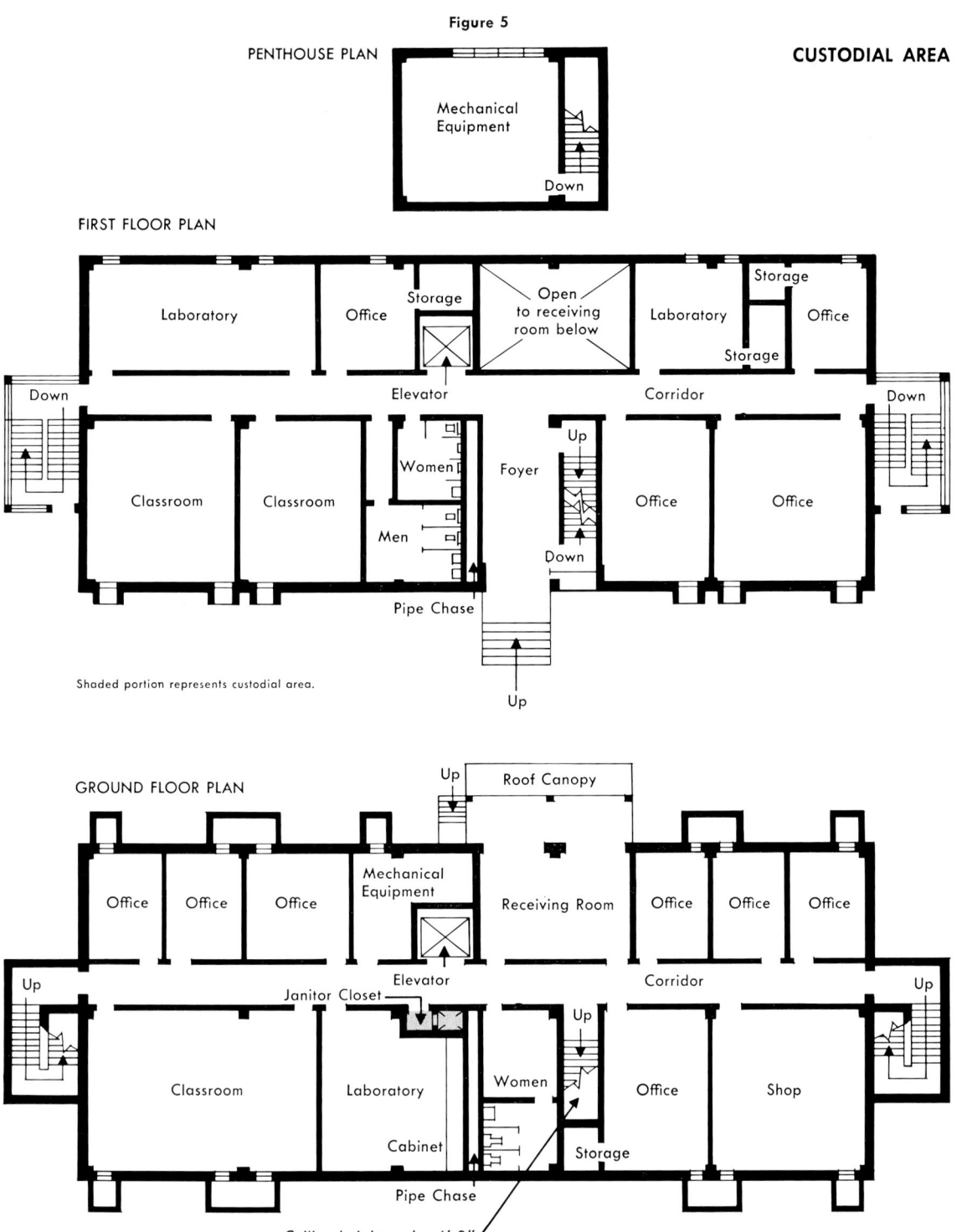

Figure 5

PENTHOUSE PLAN

CUSTODIAL AREA

FIRST FLOOR PLAN

Shaded portion represents custodial area.

GROUND FLOOR PLAN

Ceiling height under 6'-0"

14 UNIVERSITY SPACE PLANNING

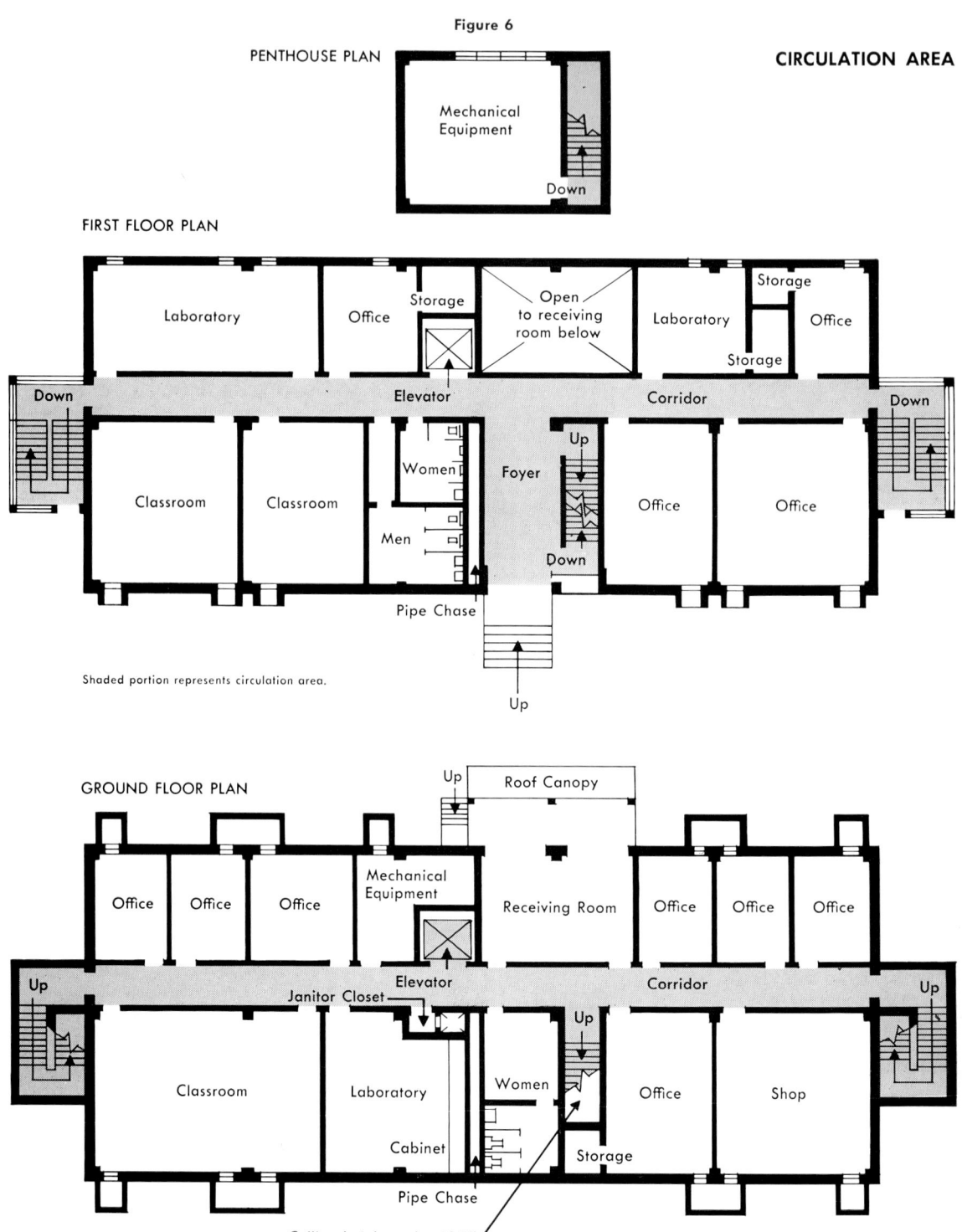

Figure 6

DESCRIPTION OF THE PLANNING PROCESS AND DEFINITION OF TERMS   15

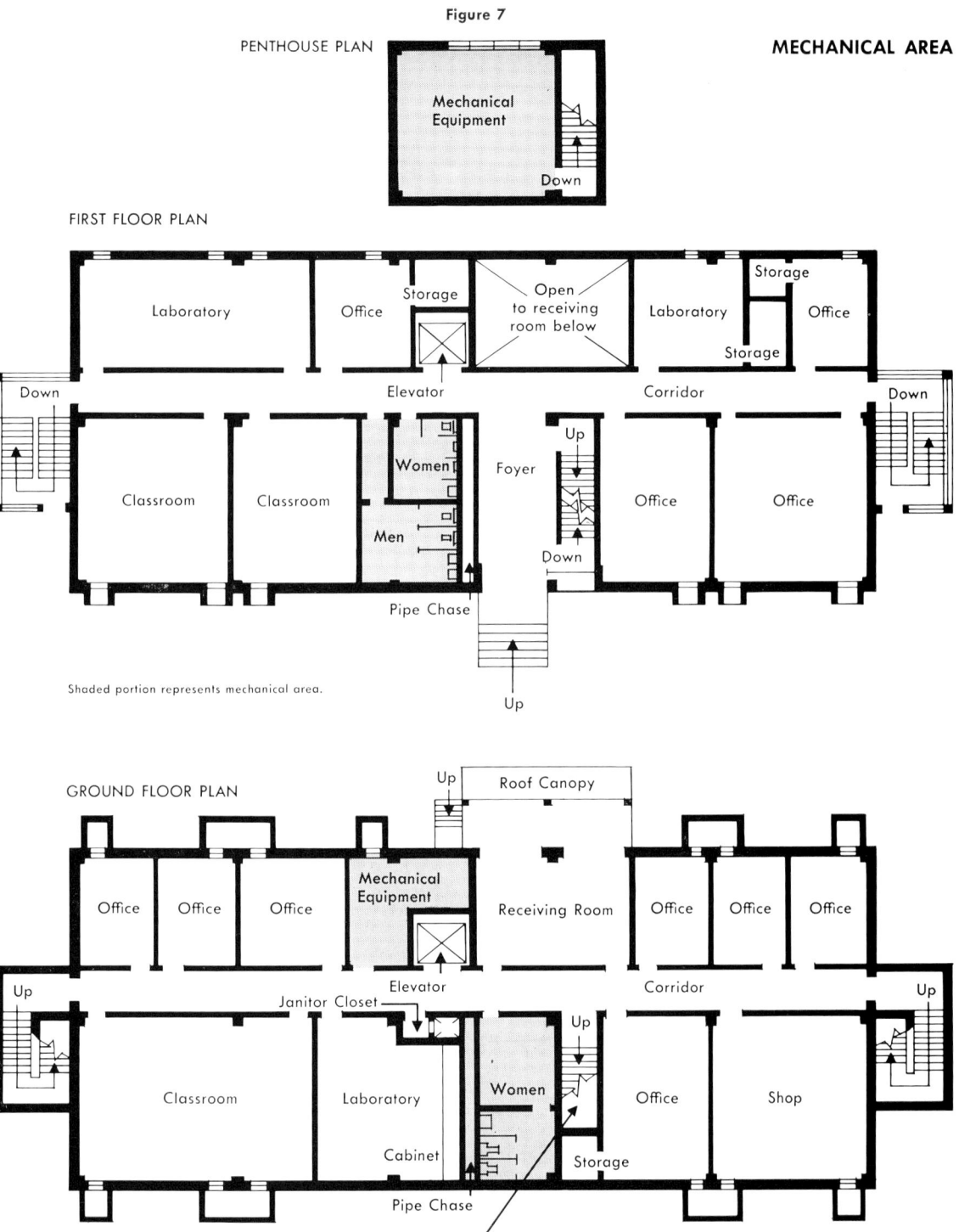

Figure 7 — MECHANICAL AREA

16 UNIVERSITY SPACE PLANNING

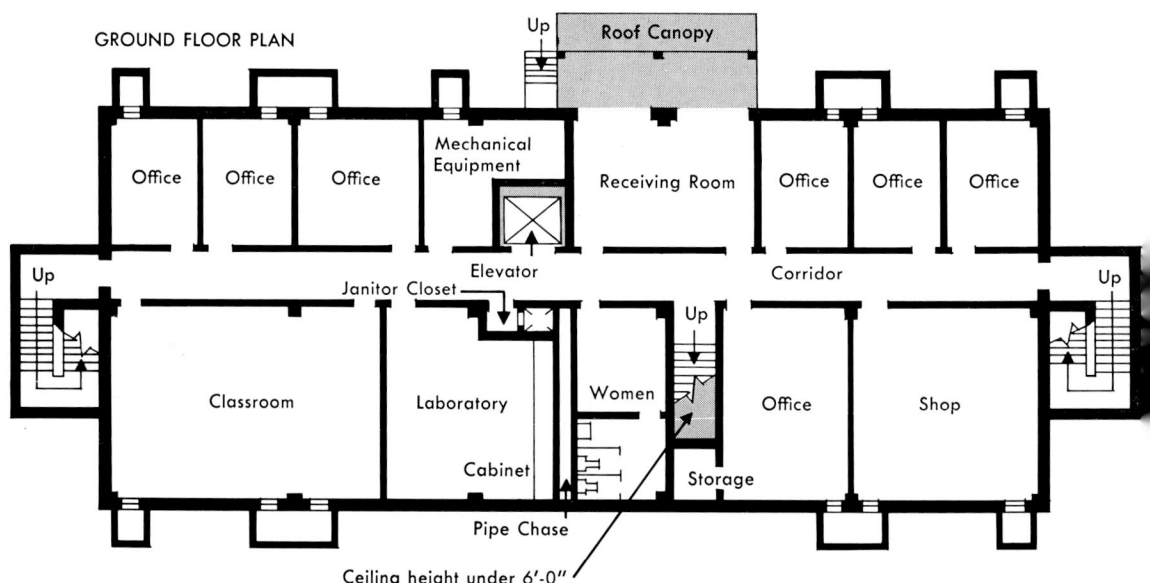

Figure 8

PENTHOUSE PLAN — CONSTRUCTION AREA

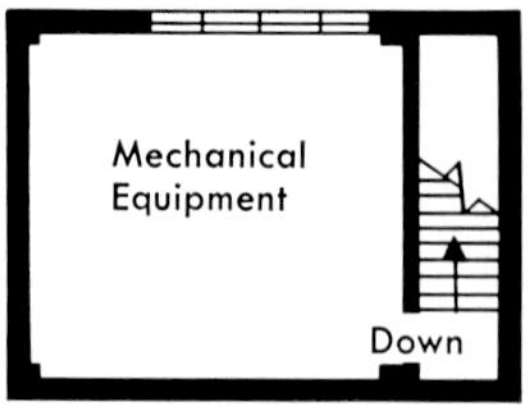

FIRST FLOOR PLAN

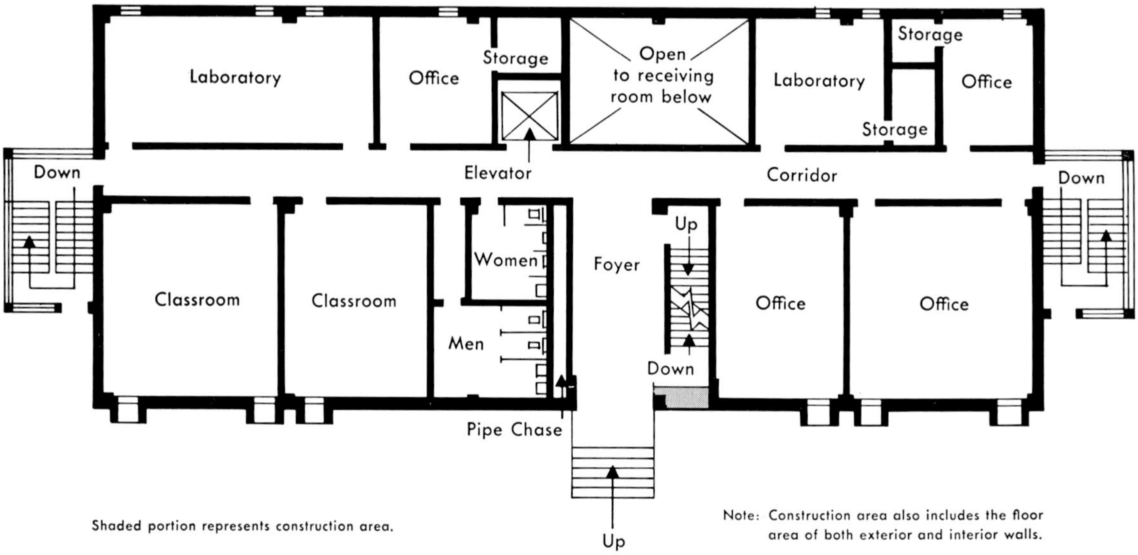

Shaded portion represents construction area.

Note: Construction area also includes the floor area of both exterior and interior walls.

GROUND FLOOR PLAN

Ceiling height under 6'-0"

TERMS USED IN UTILIZATION STUDIES AND PROJECTION OF PHYSICAL FACILITIES

Student Station. The total facilities necessary to accommodate one student for a given period of time, usually one hour. A student station may apply to a classroom, teaching laboratory, teaching gymnasium, music practice room, or other areas where a student is involved.

Period. As used in space utilization, a period is a unit of time of approximately one hour. The terms period and hour are used synonymously.

Weekly Student Hour. A unit of measure which represents one hour of instruction given to one student in one week. (As this measurement is based on a weekly effort, the utilization data of an institution on the quarter or semester system may be compared.) Some institutions use the terms student station period of occupancy, student contact hour, or student clock hour to indicate the same unit of measure.

Station Utilization. A percentage of student stations occupied when the room is in use. Some institutions use the term size ratio.

Net Assignable Square Feet per Station. The number of square feet needed to accommodate one student in the particular subject field being evaluated. In this book, the square feet per station includes support areas such as preparation rooms, balance rooms, supply rooms, and so forth.

Room Period Usage. A number of hours per week that a room is occupied by a regularly scheduled class. Some institutions use the terms weekly room hours, or weekly scheduled hours.

Square Feet per Weekly Student Hour. The number of square feet required to accommodate one student for one contact hour in a specific type of scheduled instructional space. Some institutions refer to this as a space factor. This value will be used in space projections and is a value that gives in one number an index of net assignable square feet per student station, station occupancy, and room period usage.

For example, if a classroom has 600 net assignable square feet and 30 stations, the net assignable square feet per student station would be 20 and if the room were used 30 hours per week, with a station occupancy of 67 per cent, the square feet per student contact hour would be $\dfrac{20 \text{ square feet per station}}{30 \text{ hours per week} \times .67 \text{ station utilization}}$ = 1 net assignable square foot per weekly student hour.

Building Blocks. The major space categories which form the basis for correlating the physical facilities inventory with the method of projecting physical facilities. Examples of building blocks that will be used are office, classroom, library, and so forth.

Physical Facilities Inventory. An inventory of the existing building space on campus.

Program Statement. A statement of the physical facilities to be planned giving their size, space requirement, functional relationships, and the specific requirements that should be included in a building.

Building Efficiency. The net assignable square feet in a building divided by the gross square feet.

Field of Study. Denotes an academic department or interdisciplinary unit of the institution.

Level of Student. As discussed in this book, it refers to the following levels: (These are definitions used at the University of Illinois. If these terms are used at another institution a check should be made to determine if they mean the same thing.)

Lower Division	— Freshman-Sophomore (students with less than 60 semester credit hours)
Upper Division	— Junior-Senior (students with 60 semester credit hours or more who do not have a baccalaureate degree)
Beginning Graduate	— A student admitted to graduate college who has completed less than eight units or 32 semester credit hours.
Advanced Graduate	— A student admitted to graduate college who has completed eight or more units or 32 or more semester credit hours. Usually a student with a Master's Degree or its equivalent pursuing an advanced degree or certificate.

Various institutions have different methods of determining the level of the student. As shown above, the level of student is determined by the credit hours earned, whereas in some institutions the level of student is determined on the basis of the level of instruction offered. It is not the intent of this book to discuss the pros and cons of either method, but rather to inform the reader that there are two methods and that there can be some disagreement of data between the two methods. In this book, the student level has been determined by the number of semester credit hours earned.

Student Mix. As used in this book, student mix refers to the composition of the student body by level of student. Example: a student body with 15,000 lower division; 10,000 upper division; 5,000 beginning graduates; and 2,500 advanced graduates is a 6:4:2:1 mix.

Full-Time Equivalent (FTE). A term to give the equivalence of the student body or staff of an institution on a full-time basis. It may have various values depending upon the manner in which it is defined. The exact definition and usage should be checked where any data involving an FTE are encountered.

FTE Student. FTE students, as used in the calculation of physical facilities by the "Numeric Method" in this book, are equivalent to 15 credit hours of instruction. It is the same for all fields of study and applies to all levels of students — undergraduate and graduate. In some institutions different values are used for calculating undergraduate FTE and graduate FTE. Before comparing data with another institution on an FTE basis, the method of calculating the FTE of each level of student should be checked.

INVENTORY OF PHYSICAL FACILITIES

The key to properly analyzing the existing physical facilities of any institution of higher learning is the establishment of an inventory system containing the proper data, with provisions for rearranging, reporting, and updating. With the ever-increasing number of reports on physical facilities required by federal and state agencies, the institution's procedure for collecting and processing information must be capable of supplying the data in varied formats. A space inventory consisting only of room area and department to which the space is assigned is no longer sufficient for adequate preparation of these reports. With the variety and volume of data required, it is imperative that electronic data-processing equipment be used for speed of production and dissemination of information. To be useful and effective in meeting these requirements, the inventory should have:

1. Descriptions of all facilities and their use.
2. Lists of all facilities assigned to each department or administrative unit.
3. A breakdown of the space according to the various functions of the university (teaching, research, and extension).
4. The data supplied in elements which will permit rearrangement and flexibility to produce information in the desired format.
5. Provisions for updating existing data.
6. Compatibility with the methods used in projecting space requirements.

The authors have participated in the development of a Facilities Classification and Inventory Procedures Manual that has been published by the U.S. Office of Education to facilitate comparability of reports on physical facilities to federal and state agencies. It is possible to prepare such reports from the system proposed herein by means of a conversion code. Because of the continually changing requirements of report formats, the ease of adapting this system to other formats by means of a conversion code, and the ease of communication with department heads this system affords, the authors have decided to retain the system of inventory procedures proposed here.

The elements necessary to an inventory system considered adequate to supply proper data for the various types of reports that may be requested are listed below:

1. Designation
2. Assignment
3. Area
4. Classification — usage and description
5. Categorization
6. File maintenance procedure and division of space by university function

A discussion of these elements and their relationships to the total inventory will follow.

1. The *designation element* is to contain sufficient information to enable the user to identify the specific areas to be inventoried. Usually this element contains four parts: campus identification code, building number, building name, and room number. The campus number is used when the inventory is to include physical facilities for more than one campus. A university with branch campuses will want to assign a numeric code to each of its campuses so that the electronic data-processing equipment can quickly identify the space within each of its campuses. Also, a campus identification code may be required if the inventory of an institution is involved in a state space survey.

A building number is included for ease of handling the information in the electronic data-processing equipment because numeric characters are more readily manipulated than are alphabetic characters. Therefore, it is recommended that all buildings on a campus be assigned a number. For those institutions who do not already have numbers assigned to buildings, it is suggested that a uniform numbering system be developed that will be used by everyone within the institution, particularly the physical plant department and the campus architect's office.

The building name is included in the abbreviated form to make a printout of the material more meaningful to those administrators who have to refer to such data. This eliminates having to look up the building number to make positive identification when looking at the inventory data. The abbreviation should be of sufficient length to eliminate any doubt as to which building reference is being made. See Table 1 for a sample listing of building names and their abbreviations.

For the majority of institutions, room number is the most difficult part of the designation element to secure and maintain; yet once the buildings are identified, it is the most important identification feature of a specific area. It is extremely important that each room including corridors, restrooms, janitors' closets, and mechanical rooms be assigned a specific number and that the numbering system be flexible enough to permit additional numbers in the event a

Table 1. Sample Listing of Building Codes and Abbreviations for Buildings

Bldg. Code	Bldg. Name	Bldg. Abbrev.
120	Abbott Power Plant	A P P
046	Administration Building	ADM B
028	Aeronautical Laboratory A and Brake Shoe Laboratory	ALABSL
030	Aeronautical Laboratory B	AER LB
018	Agricultural Engineering Building and Garage (South)	AG E B
183	Agricultural Engineering Research Laboratory	AG ERL
070	Agronomy Annex and Greenhouses	AGR AN
002	Agronomy Storehouse	AGR ST
026	Altgeld Hall	ALTGEL
057	Animal Genetics Building	AN GEN B
165	Animal Science Building	A S L
071	Arcade Building	ARCADE
050	Architecture Building	ARCH B
006	Armory	ARMORY
234	Armory Avenue Warehouse	AAWHSE
166	Assembly Hall	A HALL
007	Auditorium	AUDIT
004	Band Building	BAND B
158	Bevier Hall — Home Economics	BEVIER
051	Botany Annex and Greenhouses	BOT AN
169	Burnsides Research Laboratory	BUR RL
138	Burrill Hall	BURRIL
217	Central Food Stores	C F S
255	Central Receiving Warehouse	C R W
055	Ceramics Building	CERAMI
011	Ceramics Kiln House	CER KL
010	Chemistry Annex	CHEM A
024	Civil Engineering Hall	C E H
159	College of Commerce and Business Administration (West)	COMM B
167	Colonel Wolfe School	C WOLF
174	Coordinated Science and Aerospace Laboratories	CS AL
073	Dairy Manufactures Building	D M B
001	Davenport Hall	DAVENP
113	Davenport House	DAV HS
210	Digital Computer Laboratory	D C L
031	Dynamics Testing Laboratory	D T L
116	East Chemistry Building	E CHEM
160	Education Building	EDUC B
230	Educational Projects and Guidance Building — College of Education	EP GB
009	Electrical Engineering Annex	E E A
037	Electrical Engineering Building	E E B
016	Electrical Engineering Research Laboratory	EERL
015	Engineering Hall	E H
036	Engineering Research Laboratory	E R L
044	English Building	ENGL B
132	Field House — Illinois Field	FH IF
049	Filtration Plant	FIL P

room is subdivided. Renumbering as a result of remodeling usually is accomplished by inserting additional numbers into the room number sequence. However, if this is not possible because there are no numbers available, this may be accomplished by using an alphabetical prefix or suffix. To establish room numbers for institutions where none exist or an inconsistent system exists requires the cooperation of the persons in charge of the space inventory, the campus architect's office, and the physical plant department. Once all the room numbers are assigned, the responsibility of keeping the room numbering system up to date should rest with the physical plant department or campus architect's office. To help keep this inventory up to date, the inventory officer should have a set of floor plans for each building to be sure all space has been inventoried. To facilitate handling and storage, the plans are usually in a one-sixteenth-inch scale.

2. The *assignment element* of the inventory includes the name of the department or unit to whom the space is assigned and the account number assigned to that department. The department name is usually inserted in an abbreviated form. (See Table 2 for an example of abbreviations and uniform account codes.)

Table 2. Example of Uniform Code and Abbreviations

Dept. Acct. No.	Title	Abbrev.
01000	Board of Trustees	B O T
02000	President	PRES
03001	Provost	PROV
03220	Bureau of Institutional Research	B I R
04100	Accounting	ACCTG
04200	Auditing	AUDIT
04300	Bursar	BURS
04401	Purchasing	PURCH
05000	Admissions and Records	A & R
32529	Linguistics	LING
32531	Biology	BIOL
32540	Mathematics	MATH
32550	Microbiology	MCBIO
32570	Philosophy	PHIL
32609	Physiology	PHYSL
32630	Political Science	POL S
32660	Psychology	PSYCH
32681	Russian	RUSS
32682	Polish	POL
32689	Slavic Languages and Literatures	SL & L
32690	Sociology	SOC
32700	Social Science	SOC S
32721	Spanish	SPAN
32722	Italian	ITAL

The account number for each department or unit should be a uniform number which is used by the accounting division, registrar, office of institutional research, physical plant department, space inventory office, and other offices on campus that need a code number for departmental reference. This uniform account coding system usually is the first major step in establishing an integrated data system which will enable an institution to research its own activities. It is the practice at the University of Illinois to assign all general university facilities, such as classrooms, to the central scheduling office, and public corridors, circulation space, restrooms, and mechanical rooms to the physical plant department.

3. The *element used for the measurement of area* in the inventory of physical facilities is the square foot. Great care must be exercised in the taking of measurements. It is extremely important that the person assigned to this task fully understands the areas to be measured and how to take the measurements. For those institutions about to start an inventory or to update an existing inventory, it is suggested that the person assigned the task of gathering the area measurements familiarize himself with all the definitions contained in Chapter 2. It is not recommended that measurements of areas be taken from blueprints or small-scale drawings on older buildings because of the changes that may have occurred during construction or remodeling since the completion of the building. Small-scale drawings are often too inaccurate to take any kind of measurement that will have meaning. If an older institution is developing a physical facilities inventory for the first time, it is suggested that reference be made to a report titled *A Methodology for Determining Future Physical Facility Requirements for Institutions of Higher Education*.[1]

4. The *classification — usage and description* element of the inventory of physical facilities provides the major line of communication between the department and the inventorying office. The usage and description element should designate a given room in such a manner that a mental image will be given of the room, and at the same time make apparent the customary function the room serves within the university.

In many cases, a personal inspection of an area is not sufficient. For example, a person looking at a room with a table and chairs might immediately classify it as a conference room. This would be true if it were used as a conference room for a department. However, a room with the same furniture might be used for scheduled class seminars. The same room might also be used as a computation room for an instructional laboratory. In this case, it would be a laboratory auxiliary. Again, this room might be used as a group study room in the library. In this instance, the room would be a study room for the library. The terms used for describing rooms at the University of Illinois are given in Appendix A — *Facility Codes and Abbreviations Used for the Description of Space*. The terms are so descriptive that it is believed definitions are not required. The terms used to designate the customary function the room serves within the university are given below:

Office. A room or suite of rooms containing office-type equipment used by university personnel (teaching, research, administrative, extension, and "other staff") to conduct clerical, administrative, or faculty duties other than the meeting of classes. Office space also includes reception, conference, work, file, and storage areas that are required for departmental administration.

Classroom. A room that may be used by more than one department for scheduled instruction purposes. This includes those areas commonly referred to as classrooms, lecture rooms, and seminar rooms. Any storage or service rooms

---
[1] Information on this report may be obtained from the Education Research Information Center, Room 3-0-083, Maryland Avenue, S.W., Washington, D.C. 20202.

used in conjuction with the classrooms would be categorized as classroom space. (Examples are: projection booths, storage closets, preparation rooms, etc.)

There may be some question about the inclusion of rooms designated as conference rooms. The philosophy is that the designation of seminar room will mean that it is usable for general university instruction, and the designation of conference room will mean that it is for use of departmental personnel only and is to be included as office or research space for that department.

Laboratory. A laboratory is a room that has specialized equipment which normally limits its use to a single department or unit. The designation includes all space that is used for instructional laboratories, research laboratories, counseling rooms, clinic, practice rooms, art studios, pools, etc. Any storage and auxiliary service space (balance rooms, preparation rooms, etc.) necessary for the functioning of these laboratories is to be included.

Special Laboratory. A room that has specialized equipment which normally limits its use to a single department or unit, but differs somewhat from the usual first impression of a laboratory. It includes facilities such as greenhouses, animal stalls, animal retaining rooms, arenas, etc.

Library. A room or group of rooms used for the collection, storage, circulation, and use of books, periodicals, manuscripts, and other reading and reference materials, and is under administrative control of the university librarian. This includes reading rooms, carrels, stacks, faculty and student study areas. Teaching facilities for library science staff and students, although located in the library building, should be excluded from library space and classified in a manner consistent with other departments.

Auxiliary Service. All rooms and areas devoted to revenue-producing operations are to be included under auxiliary services. This includes facilities such as student union, bookstores, intercollegiate athletics, housing, and food service.

University Services. All rooms and areas that are for student or public use but are not revenue-producing will be included under university services. These services include space such as university press, stenographic service bureau area, student and faculty commons area, auditoriums and museums not used for instruction.

Physical Plant Services. All rooms and areas used for buildings and grounds maintenance other than office or warehouse space should be included under physical plant services. Included are service shops, garages, and storerooms that are above warehouse standards. Not included are mechanical areas and custodial areas.

Warehouse Space. All rooms and areas that are used for storage which are below normal building standards for heat, light, or headroom (unheated, poorly lighted, or 6 feet 6 inches or less in ceiling height) will be included as warehouse space.

Field Buildings. This category includes all space in individual buildings on university farms which are necessary for the normal operation of the farm. In general, these spaces are listed by buildings and not on a room-by-room basis.

Also, these buildings are not included in the inventory of net assignable space for instruction.

5. The *categorization element* is used to make it possible to rearrange the data into groups compatible with those normally required when reporting space inventories and space utilization to various departments and agencies.

The data provided by the classification element, which were obtained by communication with the departments and administrative units, must be reconciled with the utilization data for the scheduled instructional activities. This reconciliation requires the further subdivision of some of the usage terms for compatibility with other required reports. For example, the usage term of laboratories is further subdivided into instructional laboratories, instructional gymnasiums, pools, and drill halls, and research space. The arrangement of items in each group used to categorize the facilities is given as follows:

	Schedule No.		Schedule No.
Classrooms (Series 0100)		Auditorium, Theatre, Chapel, Assembly Hall, and Conference Rooms not Used for Instruction (Series 0600)	
Scheduled	0100		
Service	0102		
Instructional Laboratories (Series 0200)		Auditorium, Theatre, and Assembly Hall	0603
Scheduled	0200	Conference Rooms not Used for Instruction	0604
Service	1802	Exhibit Museum	0605
Hospital Rooms	1803	Office Space	0609
Greenhouse	1804		
Animal Rooms	1806	Gyms, Fields, and Armory Space not Used for Instruction (Series 0700)	
Animal Stalls	1808		
Instructional Gyms, Pools, and Drill Halls (Series 0300)		Seating and Recreation	0700
Scheduled	0300	Housing Area (Series 0800)	
Service	0302	Married Student Housing	0801
Research Space (Series 1200)		Unmarried Student Housing	0802
Research Space	1200	Group Dining Facilities	0805
Service	1802	Office Space	0809
Hospital Rooms	1803		
Greenhouse	1804	Student Service (Union, Bookstore, Lounge) (Series 0900)	
Animal Rooms	1806		
Animal Stalls	1808	Dining and Food Preparation	0902
Library Space (Series 0500)		Student Use of Union	0903
Stack Area	0502	Guest Rooms	0904
Reading and Study	0503	Commons Space in Academic Buildings	0905
Carrel Space	0504	Office Space	0909
Service Area	0506		
Office Space	0509	Campus Hospital and Health Facilities (Series 1000)	
Office Space (Series 0400)			
Office with Occupants	0401	Hospital Beds	1002
Work, Conference, and File Space	0402	Health Service	1004
Office Space and Labs	0403	Living Quarters	1005
Storage Closets and Vault	0404	Office Space	1009

	Schedule No.		Schedule No.
Buildings and Grounds Maintenance Area (Series 1100)		Athletic Association Space (Series 1400)	
Service Shops	1102	General	1400
Storeroom	1103	Office Space	1409
Warehouse	1104	Quasi-University Groups (Series 1500)	
Garage	1105		
Office	1109	General	1500
Laboratory School Space (Series 1300)		Office Space	1509
		Inactive Space (Series 1600)	
General Laboratory School	1300	Space Being Remodeled	1600
Office Space	1309	Unassigned Space	1602
		Property To Be Razed	1604
		Warehouse Space	1700

The interrelationship between the classification element and the categorization element is shown graphically in Table 3. (The description element has been deleted because of the large number of terms used.) As the subgroups within each of the categories are examined, note that all of the subgroups have similar series numbers with the exception of the instructional laboratory and research laboratory space. The reason for this inconsistency is the difficulty in separating the service areas (preparation rooms, balance rooms, shops, etc.) into proportional usage of research and instruction. The determination of the proration of these rooms to research laboratory and to instuctional laboratory is accomplished by the department head. This procedure will be explained in a later section. Note also that office space is included as a separate category in one instance and in other instances it is included with library space; laboratory school space; buildings and maintenance space; auditoriums, theatre, museum, etc. not used for instructional space; campus hospital and health service space; student service space; and housing space. The data are arranged in this manner for flexibility in reporting. In some cases, it may be desired to have the office space reported with the groupings which, in general, are not part of the academic departments or administrative units and, in other cases, it may be desired to report all office space as one entity. The data are arranged to permit reporting for either condition.

The procedure for reconciling the facilities used for formal instruction with the categorization element is outlined below.

The main portion of formal instruction, as scheduled in a timetable, will occur in the three categories of (1) classrooms, (2) instructional laboratories, and (3) gymnasiums, pools, and drill halls. There is also some instruction conducted in research laboratories, offices, special collection rooms of the library, and fields. The procedure used to determine those facilities categorized as classrooms; instructional laboratories; and gymnasiums, pools, and drill halls is one of successive selection and is given below. The following data must be available with respect to each room or space scheduled in a timetable: assignment, classification, hours per week scheduled, room, building, and area.

1. *Classrooms.* From these data, all those rooms which are assigned to the general university and have a designation as classroom usage are selected.

Table 3. Categorization

CLASSIFICATION						
		20	**CLASSROOMS** Scheduled	0100	Service	0102
		30 35	**INSTRUCTIONAL LABORATORIES** Scheduled 0200 Greenhouse 1804 Service 1802 Animal Rooms 1806 Hospital Rooms 1803 Animal Stalls 1808			
20 CLASSROOM		30 35	**INSTRUCTIONAL GYMS, POOLS, AND DRILL HALL** Scheduled 0300 Service 0302			
30 LABORATORIES		30 35 60	**RESEARCH SPACE** Research Space 1200 Greenhouse 1804 Service 1802 Animal Rooms 1806 Hospital Rooms 1803 Animal Stalls 1808			
35 SPECIAL LABORATORIES		40 10	**LIBRARY SPACE** Stack Area 0502 Service 0506 Reading and Study 0503 Office 0509 Carrels 0504			
40 LIBRARY		10	**OFFICE SPACE** Office with Occupants 0401 Work, Conference, and File Space 0402 Office Space in Laboratories 0403 Storage Closets and Vault Space 0404			
10 OFFICE	35 20 40 30 10		**LABORATORY SCHOOL** General Laboratory School 1300 Office Space 1309			
		10 55 60	**BUILDINGS AND GROUNDS MAINTENANCE** Service Shops 1102 Garage 1105 Storerooms 1103 Office 1109 Warehouse 1104			
55 PHYSICAL PLANT SERVICE		10 60 70 50	**AUDITORIUM, THEATER, MUSEUMS, ETC. NOT USED FOR INSTRUCTION** Auditorium, Theater, and Assembly 0603 Conference Rooms 0604 Exhibit and Museum 0605 Office Space 0609			
60 WAREHOUSE SPACE		30 35 70	**GYMNASIUM, FIELDHOUSE, AND ARMORY NOT USED FOR INSTRUCTION** Seating and Recreation 0700			
70 UNIVERSITY SERVICES		30 35 10 50	**CAMPUS HOSPITAL AND HEALTH FACILITIES** Hospital Beds 1002 Living Quarters 1005 Health Service 1004 Office Space 1009			
50 AUXILIARY SERVICES		40 10 60 70 50	**STUDENT SERVICE** (Union, Bookstore, Lounge) Dining and Food Preparation 0902 Student Use in Union 0903 Guest Rooms 0904 Commons Space in Academic Buildings 0905 Office Space 0909			
		10 50	**HOUSING AREA** Married Students Housing 0801 Single Students Housing 0802 Group Dining Facilities 0805 Office Space 0809			
80 FIELD BUILDINGS		60	**WAREHOUSE STORAGE SPACE** 1700			
	30 10 70 35 55 50		**ATHLETIC ASSOCIATION** General 1400 Office Space 1409			
	30 40 55 35 10 60 50		**QUASI-UNIVERSITY** General 1500 Office Space 1509			
	ALL		**INACTIVE SPACE** Space To Be Remodeled 1600 Space To Be Razed 1604 Unassigned Space 1602			

These will be analyzed as classrooms in the space utilization report and also listed as classrooms in the inventory.

2. *Instructional Laboratories.* The rooms remaining are those rooms which are either instructional laboratories; instructional gymnasiums, pools, and drill halls; research laboratories; offices; or miscellaneous areas and fields. As it is very difficult to determine whether a laboratory is a research laboratory or an instuctional laboratory at first glance, the following method is used to categorize the laboratories into instructional or research:

If a room is scheduled more than six hours per week, it is to be classified as an instructional laboratory.

If a room is scheduled six hours or less, it is to be classified as a research laboratory.

All rooms which are scheduled more than six hours per week and are listed as laboratories in the inventory will be selected. These rooms will be either instructional laboratories or instructional gymnasiums, pools, and drill halls. They may be further broken down by the description element to determine which are instructional labs and which are instructional gyms, pools, or drill halls.

3. *Research Laboratories.* The remaining laboratory rooms from step 2 will be analyzed as instruction conducted in research laboratories in the space utilization report. They will be listed with research laboratories in the inventory report.

4. *Fields.* From the remaining data, those areas which are designated as fields are to be selected. These will be analyzed as instruction conducted in fields.

5. Upon investigation, the remaining rooms will usually be departmental conference rooms, offices, special rooms in the library, etc. This space will be analyzed under the classification of instruction conducted in miscellaneous space in the space utilization reports. In the inventory report, however, they will be listed in their respective classifications.

6. *File Maintenance Procedure and Division of Space According to University Function.* At first glance, the file maintenance procedure would not appear to be an element of an inventory of physical facilities. However, the method of education is continually subject to change and as emphasis is placed upon different fields of study, it is usually necessary to do some remodeling of the existing facilities and thus change the functions and areas of rooms. If the inventory makes use of electronic data-processing equipment, it is necessary to have an updating procedure that is uniform. The procedure used at the University of Illinois will be explained in a later portion of this chapter. Whether the procedure outlined here is the one used or not is immaterial. It is necessary, however, that some procedure for revision of all elements of the inventory be provided before the inventory can be considered complete.

The second part of this element — Division of Space According to University Function — could well be a separate element. However, it is placed with the file maintenance procedure because it is believed that this is the best time for the department to review the division of space according to the university functions of teaching, research, and extension. The procedure used at the University of Illinois is to send the data on all space assigned to each department to the department head and ask for any corrections on the space as recorded. At this time, the department head is also requested to determine the manner in which the space is used percentagewise, according to the functions of teaching, research, and extension; and as to the source of funds — government, private, and university. A computer program is then written that transforms these percentages into square feet. The procedure for maintaining a space inventory for the University of Illinois and the method of file maintenance and division of space according to university function is described below:

PROCEDURES USED AT THE UNIVERSITY OF ILLINOIS FOR MAINTAINING A SPACE INVENTORY

Responsibilities

The office at the University of Illinois responsible for the maintenance of the inventory of space is the Central Office on the Use of Space. The maintenance of a current space inventory for the entire university involves certain duties and responsibilities for both the Central Office on the Use of Space and for each of the individual departments or units. The responsibilities of the Central Office on the Use of Space are:

1. To maintain the official records of space inventory.
2. To recommend assignment or reassignment of space to departments or units.
3. To supply information to aid departments in classifying space.
4. To provide information for reports on space utilization.
5. To maintain agreement of room areas as reported in the inventory with the actual size of rooms within the building.
6. To update as required to maintain a current inventory.

The responsibilities of each department or unit with respect to the space assigned to it are:

1. To check for accuracy, as to room number and area, all space assigned as per the official records.
2. To determine the classification of each room as to type and facility, and to be sure that type and facility as given agree with the actual usage of the room.
3. To indicate the functions (teaching, research, extension) conducted in each room by source of funds (government, state, private) used to accomplish the functions.

The administration of these responsibilities can only be accomplished by cooperation between the Central Office on the Use of Space and the departments or units. Although the Central Office is responsible for keeping the area of each room in agreement with the actual size of the room, the departments have the prerogative to question the accuracy of the areas on the inventory records. In these instances, the Central Office on the Use of Space will take the necessary steps to correct any errors. Whenever a department desires any information regarding the space assigned to it, it is the responsibility of the Central Office to supply the records. When a department makes a change in the use of space assigned to it, this information should be sent to the Central Office on the Use of Space. This division of responsibilities provides a check and balance between the department and the Central Office on the Use of Space, thus assuring a more accurate inventory.

Data To Be Recorded and Maintained

As mentioned, the common element of the inventory is the room number and building. Thus, all data are recorded for each room within the building. A brief review of the data required for each element of the space inventory follows:

Element	Data	Responsibility
Designation	Campus Building Room Area Occupancy Capacity	Central Office on the Use of Space (COS)
Assignment	College Department Division Dual Assignment	COS and Department
Classification	Type Facility Dual Usage	COS and Department
Functional Usage	Per Cent Teaching Per Cent Research Per Cent Extension	Department
File Maintenance Procedure	Schedule Number COS Code Year of Data	COS

Although the determination of the necessary information about each room is an important part of the space inventory, it is of no value unless it is given to the computer in a format the computer can understand. Since all information is fed into the computer by the use of IBM cards, it becomes imperative that the information gathered is punched in the IBM cards in the correct columns or fields.

The layout of the IBM card is shown on next page.

A brief explanation of each field and the method of recording the information on the worksheet for keypunching into the proper columns is presented below.

Columns 1-22 in the electronic data-processing (EDP) card are used for supplying information for the designation element. Column 1 identifies the campus for which the particular inventory is taken. Each campus is coded by a number. If there are less than ten campuses to be inventoried, only one digit field is required. If there are more than ten campuses involved, this field must be expanded to two; e.g. columns 1 and 2.

Columns 2-4 are used to indicate the building code. Since numbers are fast and easy for the computer to process, an identifying number is used for each building on each campus. The building abbreviations for each building are stored in the core of the computer. This eliminates the need for using columns of the EDP card for the building abbreviations and allows additional information to be placed on the EDP card. Although the use of alphabetic information is not necessary during the processing of the material, the alphabetic information may be brought from core storage when desired for printout of a report. See Table 1 for samples of typical building codes, names, and abbreviations.

Columns 5-10 are used to indicate the room number, including prefix or suffix where required. Columns 5-8 are basically used to indicate the room number, with column 8 being the unit position. All four of these columns must be punched on all cards. For example, room 120 would be coded 0120 to utilize all four columns; and room 3 would be coded 0003. Columns 9 and 10 are used when a room number has an alpha suffix. For example, room 165A would be coded 0165A. In this example, column 10 would remain blank. The computer program is written in such a manner that columns 9 and 10 may be left blank when the alpha designation is not used. The room number, as recorded in the inventory, should correspond with the actual number appearing on the door of the room. The university architect should be responsible for numbering each room of each building on the campus and maintaining small-scale plans containing these room numbers.

Column 11 is used to indicate that a room serves more than one function. In some cases, a part of a laboratory is used as an office. When this condition exists, an asterisk is punched in column 11, and in the example mentioned, two separate cards would be punched for the room — one showing the number of square feet assigned as laboratory and the other showing the number of square feet assigned as office.

Column 12 is used to indicate that a room is occupied by personnel from more than one department. In some cases, faculty members from two different departments may share an office. When this condition exists, a lozenge is punched in column 12, and in the example mentioned, two separate cards would be punched for the room — one showing the number of square feet assigned as office space for one department and the other showing the number of square feet assigned as office space to the other department.

Columns 13-17 are used to indicate the net assignable square feet of each room. Column 17 is the unit position. In order to avoid unnecessary errors, all columns of this field should be punched. Thus, a room with 250 square feet would be punched as 00250. The number of net assignable square feet in each room is determined from working drawings by measuring the inside dimensions of each room and calculating to the nearest square foot. If working drawings are not available, it is necessary to physically measure each room.

Columns 18-22 are used to indicate the occupancy capacity of rooms used for instruction. This number indicates the number of teaching stations in the room and is used for analyses with reference to classrooms and instructional laboratories. Again, all columns of this field must be keypunched. For example, a room with a capacity of 25 would be punched as 00025. For rooms other than those used for scheduled instruction, this field is left blank.

Columns 23-27 are used to indicate the assignment element of the inventory. This is the uniform account code identifying the departments on each campus. Again, the alphabetic information for each account code is stored in the core of the computer for the same reason as mentioned previously in the discussion of building codes. See Table 2 for a sample listing of uniform account codes, department names, and abbreviations.

Columns 28-32 are used to indicate the code numbers representing the classification of the space for each room. The code in columns 28 and 29 describes the general type of space. These are the ten items listed earlier under the classification element of the inventory system. The code in columns 30-32 describes the facility as applied to the type of space. (Appendix A gives samples of a facility code and abbreviations.) The responsibility for keeping the facility code and abbreviations current should be that of the space inventory officer. The problem of determining the type of space and type of facility for a room can be quite a difficult task. The procedure is to allow the department to make this classification, as they best know how to describe the facility they are using. In the case of inventorying a new building, the drawings should be reviewed with the departments at the time of inventory preparation.

Columns 33-68 are used to indicate the percentage division of the space by university function with respect to teaching, research, and extension, and the source of funds for support of these activities. This material will be filled in by the department head annually; more information on the completion of this portion will be supplied in a later section of this chapter.

Columns 69-72 are used to indicate the codes used for the categorization element of the inventory system. Table 4 gives the recommended schedule number, code, and the items each schedule code contains. In brief, each schedule number categorizes all similar types of space into a common group. This arrangement makes it possible to compare the actual space assigned to a department with the facility requirements generated for a department as determined by the "Numeric Method."

Table 4

Schedule Number	Card Code	Description
0100		Classrooms
	0100	Scheduled Classrooms
	0102	Service Rooms to Classrooms
0200		Instructional Laboratories
	0200	Scheduled Laboratories
0300		Instructional Gyms, Pools, Drill Halls
	0300	Instructional Gyms, Pools, Drill Halls
	0302	Service Space to Gyms, Pools, Drill Halls
0400		Office
	0401	Offices with Occupants
	0402	Work, Conference, and File Space
	0403	Office Space in Laboratories
	0404	Storage, Closets, and Vault Space
0500		Library Space
	0502	Stack Area
	0503	Reading and Study
	0504	Carrels
	0506	Service Area
	0509	Office Space
0600		Auditorium, Theatre, Chapel, Assembly Hall, and Conference Rooms not Used for Instruction
	0603	Auditorium, Theatre, and Assembly Hall
	0604	Conference Rooms not Used for Instruction
	0605	Exhibit and Museum Space
	0609	Office Space
0700		Gyms, Fieldhouse, and Armory Space not Used for Instruction
	0700	Gyms, Fieldhouse, and Armory Space not Used for Instruction
0800		Housing Area
	0801	Married Student Housing
	0802	Unmarried Student Housing
	0805	Group Dining Facilities
	0809	Office Space
0900		Student Service Space (Union Bookstore, Lounge)
	0902	Dining and Food Preparation
	0903	Student Use in Union
	0904	Guest Rooms
	0905	Lounge and Student Activity Space in Academic Buildings
	0909	Office Space

Table 4 — (Continued)

Schedule Number	Card Code	Description
1000		Campus Hospital and Health Service Facilities
	1002	Area for Hospital Beds
	1004	Area for Health Services
	1005	Area for Living Quarters
	1009	Office Space
1100		Buildings and Grounds Maintenance Area
	1102	Service Shops
	1103	Storeroom
	1104	Warehouse
	1105	Garage
	1109	Office Space
1200		Research Laboratory Space
	1200	Research Laboratory Space
1300		Laboratory School Space
	1300	General Laboratory School Space
	1309	Office Space for Laboratory School
1400		Athletic Association
	1400	General Athletic Association Space
	1409	Office Space for A A
1500		Quasi-University Groups
	1500	General Quasi Space
	1509	Office Space for Quasi Groups
1600		Space Being Remodeled, Unassigned or To Be Razed
	1600	Space Being Remodeled
	1602	Unassigned Space
	1604	Properties To Be Razed
1700		Warehouse Storage
	1700	Warehouse Storage Space
1800		Auxiliary Laboratory Space
	1802	Auxiliary Laboratory Space
	1803	Hospital Rooms
	1084	Greenhouse Space
	1806	Animal Rooms
	1808	Animal Stalls

Columns 73-76 are used to indicate the space inventory office code for ease in file maintenance. This code together with the building code and the uniform account code is used for updating any of the information within a tape system. The reason the space inventory office code is used instead of the room number is to eliminate problems arising when it is necessary to update a room which is shared by departments or which has dual facility codes. Some buildings will be so large that it is desirable to indicate the rooms by wings, such as north, south, east, and west. In these cases, the rooms may be numbered N102, S102, E102, and W102. The normal sorting procedure will not align these rooms in numeric order. By using the space inventory office code for sorting, however, it is possible to maintain the inventory in the desired number sequence within a building. It is recommended that an interval of five units between space inventory office codes be used to avoid problems of room facility splits and remodeling changes that may occur. On any building which might have additions made at a later time, it is wise to allow 300 or 400 code numbers between floors.

Columns 77 and 78 are used to indicate the last two digits of the year in which the inventory was last updated.

Columns 79 and 80 are available for more or expanded input data.

To begin the preparation of an inventory of an existing building or a new building, the first step for the space inventory officer is to obtain a set of drawings for the building and arrange a meeting with the department head. At this time, the elements of designation, assignment, classification, and file maintenance will be recorded on a worksheet. (A sample of a worksheet with this information for a given building is shown in Table 5.) The example indicates an existing building called Davenport Hall on Campus 1. It gives the area of rooms assigned to the Department of Anthropology. In conferences with the department head or his representative, the space inventory officer has determined that room 101 is an office and falls in schedule 0401, which is an office with occupants. Room 102 is determined to be a conference room as part of the department office and is given schedule number 0402. Room 103 is determined to be a teaching laboratory for scheduled instruction and is given the schedule number 0200. Room 103A is an instrument room adjacent to the laboratory and is an auxiliary to both a teaching laboratory and a research laboratory; thus, it is given the schedule number 1802. The amount of area to be distributed to teaching and research will be determined later. Room 104 is a research laboratory and is given the schedule number 1200. Originally room 104 was a laboratory of 1,080 square feet; however, the room has been divided to provide a 200-square-foot office within the room. This is given the schedule number of 0403, which is office space in laboratories. As this change was made after the original inventory was taken, the benefit of having five units between the space inventory office code numbers is apparent; it is possible to use the number 0026 as the space inventory office code for this change. Room 105 is an office with occupants and is given the schedule number 0401. After the worksheet is completed, the information is keypunched into the card and fed into the computer as part of the tape record.

The next step is to print out the tape record on a space utilization analysis form as shown in Table 6. This form is sent to the department to determine if there are any errors in the data or if any changes have occurred since the last inventory report or update was made. Information on the functional usage of each room with regard to the percentage of time each room is used for teaching, research, and extension and the source of funds for these activities is also obtained at this time. The head of the department is requested to use his best judgment in determining the percentage of time each room is devoted to these functions (teaching, research, and extension) and in checking that the total equals 100 per cent. In some instances, the division of usage of a room, such as the departmental administrative office or departmental machine shop, cannot be determined easily. These rooms are usually necessary for the operation of all

Table 5   URBANA-CHAMPAIGN BUILDING [1 / 1]   [2-4 / 001]   CENTRAL OFFICE ON THE USE OF SPACE — INVENTORY OF SPACE

Room Number (5-8)	Sub-Room (9-10)	Facility Splits* (11)	Shared Department (12)	Area Square Feet (13-17)	Occupancy Capacity (18-22)	College (23-24)	Department (25-26)	Division (27)	Type (28-29)	Facility (30-32)	Schedule Number (69-72)	COS Code (73-76)
0101				00220		32	07	0	10	070	0401	0005
0102				00360		32	07	0	10	150	0402	0010
0103				01420		32	07	0	30	130	0200	0015
0103	A			00160		32	07	0	30	737	1802	0020
0104		*		00880		32	07	0	30	130	1200	0025
0104		*		00200		32	07	0	10	070	0403	0026
0105				00180		32	07	0	10	070	0401	0030

Table 6

SPACE UTILIZATION ANALYSIS

UNIVERSITY OF ILLINOIS
CENTRAL OFFICE ON THE USE OF SPACE

BUILDING INFORMATION					SPACE ASSIGNMENT					C.O.S.	
NO.	NAME	ROOM	*□	AREA SQ FT	COLL DEPT CODE	COLL ABBREV.	DEPT ABBREV.	FACILITY CODE	DESCRIPT	CODE
001	Davenp	101		220	32070	LAS	ANTH	10070	Office	0005
001	Davenp	102		360	32070	LAS	ANTH	10150	Conf.Rm	0010
001	Davenp	103		1420	32070	LAS	ANTH	30130	Lab	0015
001	Davenp	103A		160	32070	LAS	ANTH	30737	Instrum	0020
001	Davenp	104		880*	32070	LAS	ANTH	30130	Lab	0025
001	Davenp	104		200*	32070	LAS	ANTH	10070	Office	0026
001	Davenp	105		180	32070	LAS	ANTH	10070	Office	0030

Room utilization by function columns: Teaching (Gov't, Priv, Univ), Research (Gov't, Priv, Univ), Extension (Gov't, Priv, Univ), Prorated Space (Dept, Coll, Univ), State Board Sched.

three functions — teaching, research, and extension. For conditions of this type, a fourth or prorated space column is provided. It has the subject headings of department, college, and university. If this space is that of a department, it would be listed 100 per cent under prorated space in the department column. If it is a college administrative office and is necessary for the operation of all three functions, it would be listed in the college column, etc. A computer program can be written to distribute this space over the functions of teaching, research, and extension in the same proportion as determined by the facilities assigned to the department or college for which the functional usage is known.

A question may arise regarding the completion of this form in the case of half-time graduate teaching assistants who occupy an office but also attend classes. As this office is not available to anyone except the half-time graduate teaching assistants, the procedure would be to list 100 per cent in the university column under teaching. However, if the office were occupied by a half-time graduate teaching assistant and a half-time research assistant working on university research, the procedure would be to list 50 per cent in the university column under research.

An example of the procedure for completion of Table 6 by the department head is outlined below:

As the department head checks the space assigned to him, he finds that room 105 is an office which is now shared equally with a member of the Geology Department. In correcting this line, he marks the 180 square feet down to 90 square feet for his department and notes that the office is shared equally with the Geology Department. Being satisfied that the space and the facility assignments describe the operations of the space assigned to his department, the department head can now determine the percentage of room utilization by function. In examining room 101, which is the department head's office, he prorates this as 100 per cent departmental space. Room 102 is a conference room adjacent to the department head's office, and it is also prorated 100 per cent. Room 103 is a scheduled laboratory and is used 100 per cent for university teaching. When the department head examines room 103A, he judges that it is used 50 per cent for university teaching, 30 per cent for government research and 20 per cent for university research. The laboratory portion and office portion of room 104 are used 100 per cent for government research. The office that was shared with a member of the Geology Department is used 100 per cent for university teaching. As room 105 now has dual assignment of 50 per cent to Department of Anthropology and 50 per cent to Geology, a new card must be made for room 105 showing it has a dual assignment. The completed Table 6 and the data to be keypunched into the new card are shown in Table 7. The new card is given a space inventory office code of 0031, and a lozenge is punched in column 12 denoting dual assignment. The lozenge must also be placed in column 12 of the space inventory code 0030. Thus, when the information is listed by department, the portion of room 105 that goes to Geology will be shown to be in that department. When the listing is made by

Table 7

SPACE UTILIZATION ANALYSIS

UNIVERSITY OF ILLINOIS
CENTRAL OFFICE ON THE USE OF SPACE

BUILDING INFORMATION					SPACE ASSIGNMENT					TEACHING			RESEARCH			EXTENSION			PRORATED SPACE			STATE BOARD (C/F/E)	C O S CODE
NO	NAME	ROOM	*□	AREA SQ FT	COLL DEPT CODE	COLL ABBREV	DEPT ABBREV	CODE	DESCRIPT	GOV'T	PRIV	UNIV	GOV'T	PRIV	UNIV	GOV'T	PRIV	UNIV	DEPT	COLL	UNIV		
001	Davenp.	101		220	32070	LAS	ANTH	10070	Office										100				0005
001	Davenp.	102		360	32070	LAS	ANTH	10150	Conf. Rm.										100				0010
001	Davenp.	103		1420	32070	LAS	ANTH	30130	Lab			100											0015
001	Davenp.	103A		160	32070	LAS	ANTH	30737	Instrum	50			30		20								0020
001	Davenp.	104		880*	32070	LAS	ANTH	30130	Lab				100										0025
001	Davenp.	104		200*	32070	LAS	ANTH	10070	Office				100										0026
001	Davenp.	105		~~100~~ 0090 □	32070	LAS	ANTH	10070	Office			100											0030
							Office shared equally with Geology Department																
001	Davenp.	105	□	00090	32460	LAS	GEOL	10070	Office			100											0031

buildings, both of the cards for room 105 will be shown and will fall in the order denoted by space inventory office code.

After all of this information is corrected, the necessary operations for file maintenance and the division of space according to university functions will have been completed and the computer may be programmed to supply the reports as shown below. Examples of these reports are given in Appendix B.

Inventory of Space by Building
Inventory of Space by Department
Summary of Classroom Facilities
Summary of Instructional Laboratory Facilities
Summary of Instructional Gym, Pool, and Drill Hall Facilities
Summary of Office Facilities
Summary of Library Facilities
Summary of Auditorium, Theatre, Chapel, Assembly Hall, and Conference Rooms not Used for Instruction
Summary of Gymnasium Fieldhouse and Armory Space not Used for Instruction
Summary of Housing Facilities
Summary of Student Service Facilities — Union, Bookstore, and Lounge
Summary of Campus Hospital and Health Service Facilities
Summary of Buildings and Grounds Maintenance Facilities
Summary of Research Facilities
Summary of Laboratory School Facilities
Summary of Athletic Association Facilities
Summary of Facilities for Quasi-University Units
Summary of Facilities Unassigned, To Be Remodeled, or To Be Razed
Summary of Warehouse Storage Facilities
Summary of Auxiliary Laboratory Facilities
Summary of Space Assignment to Departments by Category
Summary of Space in a Building by Category

INSTITUTIONAL DATA

It has been said that institutions of higher learning research everything but themselves. Most college and university administrators realize the importance of internal analysis, but up to this time many have not made a concerted effort to utilize institutional data necessary for proper planning. In some instances the data is available but it has not been brought together for internal analysis. It is not because the institution cannot or does not have the talent to research itself. It is simply a fact that it has not taken the time, expense, or effort to do so.

In conjunction with this observation, an article by Archie R. Ayres and John H. Russell from the Division of Higher Education, U.S. Office of Education, appeared in the April, 1964, issue of *Higher Education* titled "Organization for Administration in Higher Education."

Few colleges foresee the requirements of their expanding enterprise and design the organization for dynamic administration and growth in line with stated objectives in higher education. In general, the administrative organizations in institutions of higher education have grown up without benefit of critical attention. Once established, they have inclined the institutions toward a rigidity which is rarely adaptable to changing circumstances and special problems. Noteworthy shortcomings include: (a) Too many officers reporting to the president, (b) Student personnel interests uncoordinated and scattered among a number of officers and faculty members, (c) Academic administration not clearly identified, and (d) Scant attention given to institutional development as a discrete category of general administration. As a result, in many colleges and universities organization is an area of clearly marked weakness.

It is believed that some portion of the above statement applies to every institution of higher learning and that it is especially true when it pertains to institutional data used to analyze or plan physical facility requirements.

The statistical data gathered must be adequate to give a profile of the educational policies, procedures, and goals of the institution. These data also must be provided in a format that is adaptable to the projection of physical facilities for conditions of change in the educational program and change in the mix of the student body. As the profile of an institution is largely determined by the activities of the students and staff, it is the purpose of this chapter to indicate the type of data that will aid in translating their activities into physical facility requirements.

COURSE FACILITY FILE

A course facility file giving data regarding type of instruction, desired size of class, hours per week the class meets, and type of facility required is necessary institutional data for analyzing existing operations and projecting physical facilities. An example of the format of a course facility file for various courses in the Department of Chemistry is given below:

Dept. Code	Dept. Abbrev.	Course No.	Type of Instr.	Desired Size of Class	Hours per Week Class Meets	Type of Facility Required
32197	Chem	101	Lect	350	2	Lect Rm
32197	Chem	101	Lab	24	4	Lab
32197	Chem	101	Quiz	24	2	Classrm
32197	Chem	245	Lect	50	3	Classrm
32197	Chem	397	Lect	25	3	Classrm
32197	Chem	441	Lect-Disc	50	3	Classrm

The example of the course facility file indicates Chemistry 101 will be offered with two hours of lecture, two hours of quiz, and four hours of laboratory work per week. The total enrollments will be scheduled in section sizes of 24 for the quiz and laboratory sessions, and one lecture will be scheduled until the enrollment exceeds 350, at which time two lecture sessions will be offered. For example, if there are 600 students enrolled in Chemistry 101, two lecture sections will be required, and 25 sections of laboratory and quiz will be required. Also a need is indicated for providing four hours per week for a lecture room of 350 capacity, 50 hours per week in classrooms with a capacity of 24, and 100 hours per week in laboratories with a capacity of 24. These data are necessary for planning the required classroom facilities by size and number.

A later chapter will show an index for projecting the total classroom and laboratory facilities based on weekly student hours in the classroom and the laboratory. The course facility file provides this information. Referring back to the Chemistry 101 example, an enrollment of 600 will generate 2,400 weekly student hours in classroom and lecture facilities and 2,400 weekly student hours in laboratory facilities.

With a complete course facility file and the enrollment in each course, it is possible to determine the total weekly student hours for all scheduled instruction. From this information and additional data to be explained in the next chapter, the total area of classrooms and laboratories can be determined.

COURSE AND STUDENT-LEVEL FILE

In addition to the data supplied by the course facility file, there is a need for information on the instructional effort required by an academic department based on the courses offered. It is generally recognized that more facilities and faculty effort are required as a student progresses through his educational development. A graduate student may require a large room with research equipment for his thesis work and command almost one-fourth of the time of a faculty member; whereas a freshman may meet with 30 other students in a room the same size as the single graduate student used for his research, and the entire class may not require over one-fourth of the time of a faculty member. To account for these differences in instructional effort, four levels of student achievement are used — freshman-sophomore; junior-senior; beginning graduate; and advanced graduate. (For definitions see Chapter 2.)

The data required to establish an index of instructional effort by the departments are provided by a course and student-level file. An example of this file is given below for some chemistry courses.

				Distribution of Students by Level				
Dept. Code	Dept. Abbrev.	Course No.	Credit Hrs.	F-S	J-S	Beg. Grad.	Adv. Grad.	Total
32197	Chem	101	4	449	21	..	..	470
32197	Chem	245	3	...	27	..	..	27
32197	Chem	397	2	...	15	8	..	23
32197	Chem	441	1	...	..	19	20	39
Semester Credit Hours (SCH)				1,796	195	35	20	2,046
FTE (SCH ÷ 15)				119.73	13.00	2.33	1.33	136.40

These data may be obtained from the office of the registrar or the office of admissions and records. The measure of institutional effort is reported in terms of credit hours by level or full-time equivalent students by level of department. The use of credit hours is very straightforward and is merely the multiplication of the number of students at each level times the credit hours. For Chemistry 101 in the example above, it would be 1,796 Semester Credit Hours (SCH) for freshman-sophomore and 84 SCH for junior-senior. The FTE value is very straightforward if it is known to be derived from the student credit hour production. The FTE term has been used in many different ways in higher education, so extreme care must be exercised to make sure the reported value is the one desired.

In some cases full-time equivalent enrollment is reported by considering all of those students taking 12 credit hours or more as full-time equivalent students and adding to this number the total credit hours of those students enrolled in less than 12 credit hours divided by 12. In the case of reporting full-time equivalent students in grant applications for Title I, HEFA 1963, the procedure is to calculate the number of students by adding to the number of full-time students (those carrying at least 75 per cent of a normal student-hour load) one third of the number of part-time students. As defined in Chapter 2, *the FTE student used in the calculation by the "Numeric Method" denotes the instructional effort that is given by field of study, and is equivalent to 15 credit hours of instruction in that field.* For example, the Chemistry 101 course with 470 students meeting for four hours of credit would have 125.33 FTE (4 times 470 divided by 15). The students may be from Engineering, Agriculture, and Liberal Arts and Sciences, but the instructional effort of the 125.33 FTE is credited to the Department of Chemistry. As the example indicated, 449 were freshman-sophomore, and 21 were junior-senior; thus, the instructional effort would be 119.73 FTE under freshman-sophomore and 5.60 FTE under junior-senior. It may appear that a point is being belabored; however, much of the calculation and data for comparison with other institutions require an understanding of this basic premise.

It has been explained how the course and student-level file provides the information for determination of instructional effort required by a department. The file also serves as a useful tool in projecting instructional effort and physical facilities if the institution plans to change the mix of the student body over a period of years. In most projection procedures, it is common to "freeze the curriculum" (assume the same courses will be offered) and to calculate the physical facility requirements for the new enrollment. If the "mix" of the student body remains the same, a simple ratio of course enrollments to institutional enrollment could be made. However, if the "mix" of the student body is to change, then the ratio must be applied to the course enrollments by level of student for each course. For example, assume the following existing and projected enrollment for an institution:

Headcount Enrollment

	\multicolumn{4}{c}{Level of Student}	
	F-S	J-S	Beg. Grad.	Adv. Grad.	Total
Existing	6,000	4,000	2,000	1,000	13,000
Projected	4,000	6,000	3,000	2,000	15,000
Multiplier	0.667	1.500	1.500	2.000	

If the projected enrollment in Chemistry 101 were estimated on the basis of the institutional ratio of increase, the projected enrollment would be 542 $\left(\frac{15,000}{13,000} \times 470\right)$. However, the projected enrollment of the institution indicates a decrease in freshman-sophomore. To account for this change in "mix" the projected enrollment in Chemistry 101 should be 331 $\left(449 \times \frac{4,000}{6,000} + 21 \times \frac{6,000}{4,000}\right)$.

A comparison of the projected enrollment with the existing enrollment in the four courses of chemistry given in the example of the course and student file is given below:

Existing Enrollment

Dept. Code	Dept. Abbrev.	Course No.	Credit Hrs.	F-S	J-S	Beg. Grad.	Adv. Grad.	Total
32197	Chem	101	4	449	21	. .	. .	470
32197	Chem	245	3	. . .	27	. .	. .	27
32197	Chem	397	2	. . .	15	8	. .	23
32197	Chem	441	1	. . .	. .	19	20	39
				449	63	27	20	559

Projected Enrollment

Dept. Code	Dept. Abbrev.	Course No.	Credit Hrs.	\multicolumn{4}{c}{Distribution of Students by Level}	Total
				F-S	J-S	Beg. Grad.	Adv. Grad.	
	Multiplier			0.667	1.500	1.500	2.000	
32197	Chem	101	4	299	32	..	..	331
32197	Chem	245	3	...	41	..	..	41
32197	Chem	397	2	...	23	12	..	35
32197	Chem	441	1	...	..	29	40	69
				299	96	41	40	476

The example above indicates that although the total institution may be increasing in enrollment, the overall total enrollment in the courses listed in the above example would decrease, due to the predominance of the instruction being offered in the freshman-sophomore course. It should be noted that the projection procedures illustrated in the example are most elemental and that many institutions have projection procedures that are much more sophisticated by taking into account each class distribution by sex.

GRADUATE STUDENT DATA

In addition to the data provided by the course and student-level file, it is necessary to have information about the graduate student by level and area of study on a headcount basis. It is the opinion of the authors that research space requirements for graduate students should be calculated on a headcount basis, rather than an FTE basis. The physical facilities for the thesis research of the graduate student usually are supplied by the department in which the student is majoring. When a student begins his thesis research, he may be taking additional courses in other departments. As research is nearing completion, the graduate student may be registering all his effort in the major department. If the research calculations were based on FTE by departments, the departments in which he is taking course work would be generating a need for research space. If the research calculations were based on a headcount by major, the necessary research space would be generated in the correct department. Usually students beginning graduate work spend their early semesters in course work and require very little research space. Whereas the advanced graduates, having completed about eight units or 32 semester credit hours, start to work on their theses and require facilities for their research setup. The data on headcount graduate students can usually be obtained from the registrar's office or from the graduate college. The suggested format for obtaining these data is shown below.

Alphabetical Listing of Graduate Headcount Data by Major Department

Student S.S. No.	Name	Major Dept.	Accumulated Units[a]	Beg. Grad.	Adv. Grad.
123456789	Able, James	Chem	6.00	1	
234567890	Baker, Fred	Chem	29.00		1
345678901	Charles, John	Chem	20.00		1
356789012	Jones, Don	Chem	7.00	1	
456789012	Smith, John	Chem	16.00		1
				2	3

Total Graduate Students 5
Total Beginning Graduates 2 ; Advanced Graduates 3

[a] 1 unit = 4 semester credit hours.

Alphabetical Listing of Graduate Headcount Data by University

Student S.S. No.	Name	Major Dept.	Accumulated Units	Beg. Grad.	Adv. Grad.
345678901	Adams, Ray	Geog	12.00		1
123456789	Able, James	Chem	6.00	1	
234567890	Baker, Fred	Chem	29.00		1
365432101	Barnes, Charles	Agr. Ec.	3.00	1	
345678901	Charles, John	Chem	20.00		1
376543210	Dillon, James	Unclass	8.00		1
356789012	Jones, Don	Chem	7.00	1	
387654321	Moore, Robert	French	22.00		1
456789012	Smith, John	Chem	16.00		1

The first listing gives the graduate students in the Department of Chemistry. Based upon the definitions of beginning graduates and advanced graduates in Chapter 2, Mr. Able, who has 6.00 units, would be recorded as a beginning graduate. Mr. Baker, who has 29.00 units, would be recorded as an advanced graduate.

The second listing of the graduate students by the university is not absolutely required, but it has been found that a listing of this type is very useful. Because of the possibility of errors in the listing of the graduate students by major departments, the first listing should be sent to the department head for review and correction. The alphabetical listing of the graduate headcount data by university provides a very useful tool when determining if the corrections have been made by all departments. In some graduate institutions, there may be some students who have not declared a major. These students will generate institutional effort but should not generate research space, because students who have not declared a major will not be doing thesis research.

Some graduate students have been granted fellowships. These fellowships may be university fellowships that are supported through outside donors. The institutional policy may indicate a desire to provide this student with desk space in an office. If it is the institutional policy to provide any special physical facilities for fellowship students, it will be necessary to provide data similar to the graduate headcount by major department and university. It may be possible to gather it at the same time.

FACULTY DATA

Data for faculty activities are usually available, as almost all institutions have a faculty statistical report or a faculty service report form. The main use of the faculty data will be to determine the FTE that generates office space, research space, and library space in the calculation of physical facility requirements by the "Numeric Method." In the "Numeric Method," all academic positions will generate office space; however, only those faculty members engaged in teaching or research will generate research and library carrel space. It is assumed that all research assistants and teaching assistants are graduate students and will generate research space as graduate headcount students and will not generate research space as members of the faculty. This requires teaching and research assistant data to be separated from the other faculty data. All data regarding faculty activities are to be gathered in terms of FTE with FTE being stated as a per cent appointment of a faculty member.

The data to be gathered regarding the faculty activities for the generation of research and library space are the FTE teaching staff less the teaching assistants; the FTE teaching assistants; the FTE research staff less the research assistants; the FTE research assistants; and the other FTE faculty involved in counseling, administration, extension, etc. A suggested format to collect data on faculty activities is given below.

Data on Faculty Activities

Employee Number	Name	Dept. Acct. Number	Per Cent Appointment	FTE Teaching Staff Less Teaching Assistants	FTE Teaching Assistants	FTE Research Staff Less Research Assistants	FTE Research Assistants	FTE Other	Total Faculty Less Teaching and Research Assistants
(1)	(2)	(3)	(4)	(5)	(6)	(7)	(8)	(9)	(10)
344-24-5602	Able, John	31416	0.50		0.50				
362-71-8301	Baker, Sam	31416	1.00	0.50		0.50			1.00
346-54-3210	Card, James	31416	1.00					1.00	1.00
362-78-9102	Chow, Shad	31416	0.50				0.50		
Total			3.00	0.50	0.50	0.50	0.50	1.00	2.00

This information is to be gathered on a departmental or unit basis and then summarized by college or university as desired. The example gives data on faculty activities for a department which has a uniform account code of 31416 and indicates that for the three FTE staff involved, Mr. Able is on a half-time teaching assistant appointment; Mr. Baker is on a full-time appointment, but spends 50 per cent of his time teaching and 50 per cent of his time doing research; Mr. Card is on a full-time appointment and is performing duties other than teaching or research, maybe in the area of counseling or administration; and Mr. Chow is on 50 per cent appointment and is a research assistant. From a form such as that illustrated above, it is possible to obtain the necessary data on staff by FTE to make the necessary physical facility requirement calculations.

The initial premise for determining office space requirements is that if a person is not on the payroll, he should not generate office space. It does not necessarily follow that if a person is on the payroll, he should have office space. There are many persons, such as physical plant maintenance personnel and laboratory technicians, who do not require office space. In general, most institutions have a position code for the academic and nonacademic personnel. This is especially true of institutions having a civil service system. The usual procedure is to use the payroll for a department or unit and, by means of the position code, determine whether a person needs an office. After this determination has been made, the record is sent to the department for review and approval. A suggested format for this procedure is shown below.

Data to Obtain Office Space Requirements

Employee Number	Dept. Acct. Number	Name	Position Code	FTE Not Requiring Office	FTE Faculty Requiring Office	FTE Nonacademic Requiring Office
344-34-5602	31416	Able, John	R089		0.50	
345-67-7904	31416	Adams, Marie	3243			1.00
362-71-8301	31416	Baker, Sam	R081		1.00	
354-67-8213	31416	Bloom, Marie	0846			1.00
346-54-3210	31416	Card, James	2601	1.00		
357-44-6213	31416	Charles, Ben	R082		1.00	
362-78-9102	31416	Chow, Shad	R089		0.50	

The example indicates that Mr. Able is a faculty member on 50 per cent appointment. Marie Adams is a nonacademic person (secretary) on full-time 100 per cent appointment; Mr. Baker is a professor on 100 per cent faculty appointment; Mrs. Bloom is a nonacademic person (clerk-typist) on 100 per cent appointment; Mr. Card is a nonacademic employee (instrument maker) on 100 per cent appointment and does not require office space. Mr. Charles is an associate professor on 100 per cent appointment. Mr. Chow is a graduate assistant on 50 per cent appointment. For the seven people listed above, office space is generated by five FTE. It has been advantageous to have a complete alphabetical listing of all persons on the payroll for checking the possibility of an error or for verifying conditions in which a faculty member holds an appointment with two different departments. It will usually be determined that the man will have his office in only one department, and the entire FTE will be given to that department for the generation of office space. When a payroll form is sent to a department for review, corrections can be made and cross-checking can be done by means of an alphabetical listing. A suggested format of an alphabetical listing is shown below.

Employee Number	Name	Department Account Number	Position Code	FTE Appointment
344-62-7431	Jackson, Richard	22225	R089	0.50
344-75-6214	Jones, Donald	31560	R081	0.35
344-75-6214	Jones, Donald	44410	R081	0.15
344-75-6214	Jones, Donald	44430	R081	0.50

In the above example, Mr. Jones is on 100 per cent appointment but his time is divided 35 per cent with department 31560, 15 per cent with department 44410, and 50 per cent with department 44430. In the data on faculty activities, he would be listed in each of the departments by the percentage of appointment in that department; however, conditions may be that he has an office only in department 31560. In this case, one FTE would be allocated to department 31560 for office space, and the other two departments would receive no credit for office space for Mr. Jones.

LIBRARY DATA

To calculate the amount of library stack required at an institution, the existing number of volumes must be known. Only those volumes and materials such as maps, aerial photographs, microfilm reels, etc. in the central library and branch libraries under control of the library administration are to be counted. Departmental and individual collections not under the direction of the central library administration are not to be included. Usually, these latter collections are quite small and are contained in the conference or office space of the department.

PROJECTING FUTURE STAFF REQUIREMENTS

To this point a procedure for gathering institutional data has been presented for:

1. The projection of enrollments in the course offerings of an institution when the student mix changes.
2. The determination of weekly student hours to be conducted in classrooms and laboratories.
3. The determination of the instructional effort in each department for each level of student.
4. The determination of the staff activities.

It is generally believed that more staff are required per FTE student as the level of the student increases. If this be true, some method of projecting staff requirements by level of student must be applied if the student mix changes at the institution. If it is planned to keep the student mix constant and the curricula offered in the institution relatively the same, a determination of the student-staff ratio is not important as the staff should increase proportionally to the enrollment increase. However, the educational planning of most states has been to have those existing institutions within the state plan on taking more graduate students, thereby changing the student mix. For conditions such as these it is necessary to evaluate the student-staff ratios by level of student and translate the ratio into values that can be used for projection purposes. The exact student-staff ratio for a department will depend upon the educational program and the philosophies of the institution and thus no staffing formula will be proposed by the authors. To illustrate a procedure for projecting future staff requirements, a hypothetical student-staff ratio and enrollment pattern is given for a hypothetical department. If the desired student-staff ratio for the department were one FTE staff for 18 FTE freshman-sophomores, one FTE staff for 12 junior-seniors, one FTE staff for every nine beginning graduates, and one FTE staff for every four advanced graduates, a multiplier for projecting staff increases for any specific enrollment increase could be obtained as follows:

$$\text{Staff Multiplier} = \frac{\dfrac{\text{Projected FTE Enrollments by Level}}{\text{Staffing Ratio by Level}}}{\dfrac{\text{Existing FTE Enrollments by Level}}{\text{Staffing Ratio by Level}}}$$

If the existing and projected enrollment for the department were as given below, the staff multiplier would be 1.245.

	F-S	J-S	Beg. Grad.	Adv. Grad.	Total
Existing Department FTE Enrollment	420	368	56	40	884
Projected Department FTE Enrollment	367	549	70	54	1040

$$\text{Staff Multiplier} = \frac{\dfrac{367}{18} + \dfrac{549}{12} + \dfrac{70}{9} + \dfrac{54}{4}}{\dfrac{420}{18} + \dfrac{368}{12} + \dfrac{56}{9} + \dfrac{40}{4}} = 1.245$$

The above calculation indicates the present staff would have to be increased by 24.5 per cent. This is in contrast to a 17.6 per cent enrollment increase $\left(\dfrac{1040-884}{884} \times 100\right)$. This illustrates the effect that increasing the level of student has on staff requirements which in turn will generate a need for additional research and office space.

With all of the above information formulated or gathered, the individual responsible for planning is now in a position to apply the institutional data input to the appropriate space standards.

5

PROJECTION OF PHYSICAL FACILITIES BY THE "NUMERIC METHOD"

The general philosophy of the "Numeric Method" for determining space requirements is that physical facilities of an institution of higher learning can be grouped into categories. These categories are referred to as the "building blocks" of the institution, and for each of the major "building blocks" there exists an index for determining the amount of space required. The amount of space required for each of these "building blocks" will depend upon the enrollment, the educational activity by level of student, and the fields of study offered.

The purpose of the "Numeric Method" is twofold: (1) to present a logical system for the calculation of space requirements and (2) to present space standards that should be usable for most institutions of higher learning. The methodology is by far the most important feature to be presented. However, the space standards presented will serve to form boundary conditions for the purposes of presenting capital budget requests and planning new projects. It is recognized that in every institution there will be instances where special circumstances will warrant adjustment in the standards. This is to be expected as certain departments, although having the same name, may have completely different educational goals.

The "building blocks" that define the physical facilities of an institution are classroom, instructional laboratory, instructional gym, office, research laboratory, archive and research equipment storage, library, commons, physical plant, student services, health service, inactive space, auditorium and museum (not used for instruction) and gymnasium (not used for instruction). The remainder of the chapter will discuss the methodology and space standards for each of the "building blocks."

CLASSROOM

This classification includes those spaces commonly referred to as classrooms, lecture rooms, seminar rooms, and the auxiliary support facilities such as preparation areas and projection booths. The function of this "building block" is to provide a facility that will allow an instructor to meet with a group of students for a lecture and/or recitation. Therefore, the index for the projection and analysis of classroom space should be based upon the number of weekly student hours in classrooms required for the educational program and the area required per weekly student hour.

The area per weekly student hour is derived from three values: (1) the area required for the student station; (2) the number of hours per week classrooms are to be scheduled; and (3) the percentage of time each station is to be occupied when the classroom is in use.

The number of square feet per station will vary with the size of the room and type of station used. In large lecture halls using auditorium-type seating, nine square feet is usually sufficient; however, in a seminar room, 18 to 20 square feet may be required. Generally speaking, it can be stated that in classrooms, the larger the number of stations, the smaller the square feet per station. When considering the auxiliary space needed with a classroom, it was found in a survey[1] that the station size ranged from 12.4 to 19.8 square feet with a weighted mean of 14.7. It is recommended that for the projection and evaluation of classroom space, a station size of 15 square feet be used. Because of certain educational program requirements, some institutions may wish to vary from the recommended value of 15. However, some justification should be presented for any changes of more than one square foot per station.

The number of hours per week classrooms are to be scheduled is a matter of policy. It may be institutional, or in those states having a Board of Higher Education which governs utilization of physical facilities of public institutions, it becomes a state-wide policy. To assure the use of existing facilities, some institutions have adopted, as a matter of policy, the number of hours per week classrooms must be scheduled before new classroom space is to be requested. The majority of those institutions having established such a policy have selected 30 hours per week as an optimum standard. This standard applies only to the daytime schedule (usually 7 A.M. to 5 P.M.), with night classes considered beyond the standard. If, however, the classroom demand is heavier in the night program than in the daytime, the nighttime program would govern the quantity required.

There are a few institutions, because of their geographical locations and educational programs and policies, who have set a standard as high as 36 hours

---

[1] *State-Wide Space Survey: A Survey of the Amount and Utilization of Nonresidential Space Available for Higher Education in Illinois* (Illinois Board of Higher Education, 300 East Monroe Street, Springfield, Illinois, 1965), p. 23.

per week usage of their classrooms. This is considered maximum and not attainable by most colleges and universities during the daytime schedule. Inquiries and surveys have revealed that the proposed usage of classrooms ranges between 30 and 36 hours per week. It is recommended that a value of 30 be used.

The percentage of time each station is occupied when the classroom is in use tends to vary quite widely in some institutions because the educational program and the educational policies do not coincide with the number and size of classrooms available. Inquiries have tended to indicate that 60 per cent station utilization is optimum for daytime use — 7 A.M. to 5 P.M. A survey[2] reveals that the station utilization ranges from 45.3 to 74.3 with a weighted mean of 57.3 per cent. It is recommended that a standard of 60 per cent student station use be adopted for the projection of classroom space.

The method of arriving at an index which indicates the value of the square feet per weekly student hour using the values recommended is shown as follows:

$$\text{Square feet per station} = 15$$
$$\text{Hours per week classrooms are to be used} = 30$$
$$\text{Per cent of time each station is occupied when the classroom is in use} = 60$$
$$15 \div (30 \times .60) = .833$$

If, however, it is decided to use a combination of values other than those recommended, the "Numeric Method" makes it possible to substitute other values into the equation shown above in determining the number of square feet per weekly student hour.

The above index of .833 indicates the quantity of classroom space in square feet per weekly student hour that should be available at any given time for the educational program. It does not indicate the size of the classrooms that should be constructed. A determination of the size of classrooms to be built can easily be analyzed from historical data gathered by the institution and from the course facility file. An analysis of the class sizes for the previous years and a constant monitoring of changes in teaching techniques by the departments through updating of the course facility file will indicate the classroom sizes needed. This should be compared with the number of existing classrooms in each size range.

INSTRUCTIONAL LABORATORY

Instructional laboratory space serves the same objective as classroom space; however, this type of space usually contains equipment or is so arranged that use is restricted to a particular field of study. The method for computing the index for determination of instructional laboratory space is the same as for classrooms; namely, weekly student hours in instructional laboratories and the area per weekly student hour. However, unlike classrooms, the area required per weekly student hour in instructional laboratories will vary, depending upon the field of study to be served. In addition to the area required for the stations

[2] *State-Wide Space Survey*, p. 28.

actually occupied by the student in the laboratory, there will be some auxiliary space required for storerooms, preparation rooms, balance rooms, etc. The total area per station including auxiliaries may vary from slightly more than 15 as in classrooms to 160 square feet. For example, a student station in the chemistry laboratory may require 50 square feet, but an additional 18 square feet may be required for auxiliary space of balance rooms and storerooms; whereas in a drafting room only 32 square feet may accommodate the station and the auxiliary storage space required.

Normally, a laboratory will be used fewer hours per week than a classroom due to the inability to obtain flexibility in scheduling, but the student stations will usually be better utilized when the room is occupied due to a more uniform class size. Inquiries and surveys have revealed that institutions that have adopted standards for instructional laboratories use either 20 hours per week with 80 per cent student station utilization or 24 hours per week with 80 per cent student station utilization. If 20 hours per week were used for a laboratory which required 68 square feet per station, a value of 4.25 square feet per laboratory contact hour would be obtained [68 ÷ (20 × .80) = 4.25]. If the institution had adopted a standard for instructional laboratories of 24 hours per week with 80 per cent station utilization, the square feet per contact hour would change from 4.25 to 3.54. Table 8 indicates the recommended square feet per weekly student hour required by field of study for 20 hours per week and 24 hours per week with an 80 per cent student station utilization.

In addition to the above listed instructional laboratories, most universities have music practice rooms, language listening laboratories, and program teaching laboratories. The methodology for computing the space for these three types of laboratories is the same as for the instructional laboratories listed above; however, utilization will be different. Music practice rooms usually range in station size from 60 to 100 square feet. These rooms should be scheduled on an average of 48 hours per week. Because each room is equivalent to a single station, the student station utilization will be 100 per cent. Therefore, for a station size of 80 square feet, the recommended square feet per weekly student hour is 1.67 [80 ÷ (48 × 1.00) = 1.67].

Language listening laboratories and programmed teaching laboratories also should be used on an average of 48 hours per week. However, like the regular instructional laboratories, the student station utilization should average 80 per cent. The recommended student station size is as follows:

Language listening laboratories   25 square feet
Programmed teaching laboratories   55 square feet

Therefore, the recommended square feet per weekly student hour is:

.65 [25 ÷ (48 × .80) = .65] for language listening laboratories
1.43 [55 ÷ (48 × .80) = 1.43] for programmed teaching laboratories.

It is recognized that when a small number of weekly student hours are generated, an institution cannot construct a partial laboratory; therefore, the institution must construct the laboratory in the desired size. By doing this, the university should recognize that this laboratory has a capacity for additional

Table 8. Instructional Laboratory Requirements

		Net Assignable Square Feet per Weekly Student Hour	
Field of Study	Net Assignable Square Feet per Station Including Auxiliaries	20 Hours per Week; 80 per Cent Station Utilization	24 Hours per Week; 80 per Cent Station Utilization
Agriculture			
Agriculture Engineering	160	10.00	8.33
Agronomy	70	4.38	3.64
Animal Science	160	10.00	8.33
Dairy Science	68	4.25	3.54
Food Science	96	6.00	5.00
Forestry	65	4.06	3.39
Home Economics	100	6.25	5.21
Horticulture	65	4.06	3.39
Plant Pathology	65	4.06	3.39
Commerce and Business Admin.			
Accountancy	32	2.00	1.67
Business Education	32	2.00	1.67
Economics	32	2.00	1.67
Finance	32	2.00	1.67
Business Administration	32	2.00	1.67
Industrial Administration	32	2.00	1.67
Marketing	32	2.00	1.67
Education			
Education Administration and Supervision	32	2.00	1.67
Educational Psychology	65	4.06	3.39
Elementary Education	32	2.00	1.67
History and Philosophy of Education	32	2.00	1.67
Secondary and Continuing Education	32	2.00	1.67
Vocational and Technical Education	65	4.06	3.39
Engineering			
Aeronautical and Astronautical Engineering	160	10.00	8.33
Ceramic Engineering	112	7.00	5.83
Civil Engineering	112	7.00	5.83
Electrical Engineering	65	4.06	3.39
General Engineering	32	2.00	1.67
Mechanical Engineering	160	10.00	8.33
Industrial Engineering	160	10.00	8.33
Mining Engineering	160	10.00	8.33
Metallurgy Engineering	160	10.00	8.33
Petroleum Engineering	160	10.00	8.33
Nuclear Engineering	160	10.00	8.33
Physics	65	4.06	3.39
Theoretical and Applied Mechanics	160	10.00	8.33
Fine and Applied Arts			
Architecture	65	4.06	3.39
Art[a]	60	3.75	3.13
Band	48	3.00	2.50
Landscape Architecture	65	4.06	3.39
Music Laboratories	48	3.00	2.50
Theater	100	6.25	5.21
Urban Planning	65	4.06	3.39

Table 8 — (Continued)

Field of Study	Net Assignable Square Feet per Station Including Auxiliaries	Net Assignable Square Feet per Weekly Student Hour 20 Hours per Week; 80 Per Cent Station Utilization	24 Hours per Week; 80 Per Cent Station Utilization
Journalism			
Advertising	48	3.00	2.50
Journalism	48	3.00	2.50
Radio and TV	96	6.00	5.00
Liberal Arts and Sciences			
Anthropology	50	3.13	2.60
Astronomy	50	3.13	2.60
Botany	50	3.13	2.60
Chemistry	68	4.25	3.54
Entomology	50	3.13	2.60
Geography	68	4.25	3.54
Geology	68	4.25	3.54
Microbiology	68	4.25	3.54
Physics	65	4.06	3.39
Physiology	68	4.25	3.54
Psychology	50	3.13	2.60
Sociology	30	1.88	1.56
Speech	32	2.00	1.67
Zoology	50	3.13	2.60
Library Science	48	3.00	2.50
Physical Education			
Physical Education for Men	250	11.00[b]	
Physical Education for Women	250	11.00[b]	
Recreation	32	2.00	1.67
Health and Safety	64	4.00	3.33
Dance	250	11.00[b]	
Armed Forces[c]			
Air Force Science	32	2.00	1.67
Military Science	32	2.00	1.67
Naval Science	32	2.00	1.67

[a] Studios calculated with research space requirements.
[b] Usage based on facilities being scheduled as well as classrooms from 7 A.M. to 4 P.M. and 80 per cent station utilization.
[c] Drill Hall not included.

weekly student hours and no consideration should be given to adding more laboratory space until the excess capacity is utilized. The capacity of a particular laboratory can be computed from the above components of the instructional laboratory index.

OFFICE SPACE

This space may be defined as a room or suite of rooms containing office equipment used to conduct clerical, administrative, or faculty duties other than meeting of classes. Office space includes reception areas, conference areas, and work and file storage areas required by administrative units. The amount of office space any institution generates will depend upon the philosophies and standards of the university. Some institutions have standards of office size dependent upon the rank of the faculty. Others prefer single-station offices to multiple-station offices and vice versa. After examining many different standards, it is believed the best method of calculating office space is to base the office space requirements upon the full-time equivalent faculty and staff members requiring office space and to establish a standard amount of office space per FTE. By calculating office space in this manner, the total office space requirements may be generated. Then the office space arrangement can be planned by the department and the architect within these boundary conditions, taking into account the building module, the desire for single- or multiple-station offices, and the reception, file, and conference areas.

The minimum amount of space recommended for each FTE staff member requiring office space is 135 square feet. In general the allowance of 135 net assignable square feet (NASF) per FTE provides private offices of 120 square feet for the faculty, a larger office for the department head, conference rooms, reception areas, and file and work rooms for the departmental offices. The allowance of 135 square feet per FTE generates sufficient office space to provide these facilities when the number of FTE staff requiring office space is above 25; when the FTE is below 25 certain special allowances must be granted.

When a department has 1 to 5 FTE requiring office space, the 135-square-foot allowance is believed adequate for the necessary private offices and a larger office for the department head, which may also serve as a conference room. However, there does not appear to be adequate space generated to provide a reception area. Thus, an allowance of 120 NASF is added for a reception area.

When a department has 6 to 15 FTE requiring office space, the 135-square-foot allowance is believed adequate for the items mentioned above but not adequate for a conference room to accommodate 8 to 10 persons. Thus, an allowance of 200 NASF is added for a conference room.

When a department has 16 to 25 FTE requiring office space, the 135-square-foot allowance is adequate for the above mentioned items including a conference room for 8 to 10 persons, but it is not adequate for a slightly larger conference room, which may be required. Thus an allowance of 50 NASF is added for a larger conference room.

A summary of the additional allowances for small departments follows:

1. Departments with 0 to 5 FTE requiring office space — add 120 NASF to allow for reception room.
2. Departments with 6 to 15 FTE requiring office space — add 200 NASF to allow for conference room.
3. Departments with 16 to 25 FTE requiring office space — add 50 NASF to allow for conference room.

In the calculation of FTE's generating office space, it may be institutional policy to add office space for emeriti professors and fellows. At the University of Illinois, an allowance of 0.5 FTE is made for each emeritus professor and 0.4 FTE for each fellowship student for which the department wishes office space. In administrative departments where there are large numbers of clerical personnel and a high file and records requirement, such as the admissions and records office or the business office, the active files and records can be accommodated within the 135 NASF because clerical personnel can be accommodated in less than 75 square feet per FTE. Another administrative unit that should be contained within the office space standards is the administrative data-processing unit if office space is generated for the keypunch operators and machine operators. The space requirements generated will be sufficient for the keypunch machines and computers.

RESEARCH SPACE

Research space is the space required for individual investigative work. For most institutions this type of space is very difficult to evaluate, as it involves space requirements for types of activities that are not predictable. When a person attempts to translate this portion of an educational program into square feet, he will usually be accused of stifling research development or creating mediocrity through a space-leveling formula. Some criteria must be used for determining the space requirement for this "building block," however, because this type of space can amount to as much as 25 per cent of the total academic space in some institutions. It should be restated that the purpose for projecting research space, as well as the other types of space, is to establish a boundary condition within which to work. This allows the department head and/or dean to allocate the research space to the individuals on the basis of productive research programs. It must be understood that the procedure proposed is a method of projecting the space needs of a department and, in turn, of an institution. It is not a procedure by which space is to be assigned or allocated to individual faculty members or graduate students.

A method utilizing the "research demand unit" concept has been developed. The research demand unit (RDU) concept is based on the premise that research space is generated by the FTE research faculty, FTE teaching faculty, and headcount graduate students by level of (a) beginning graduates and (b) advanced graduates.

It is recognized that the FTE research faculty require more research space than the FTE teaching faculty. The FTE research faculty devote 100 per cent of their time to research, whereas the FTE teaching faculty are expected to devote approximately 20 per cent of their time to research. In addition, the advanced graduate student devotes more of his time to individual research than does the beginning graduate student, whose time is devoted mainly to scheduled classes, seminars, and library research. To account for the variation in activities, the following research demand units are proposed:

	Research Demand Units
FTE Research Faculty	15
FTE Teaching Faculty	3
Headcount Beginning Graduates	3
Headcount Advanced Graduates	15

It must be stressed that only those faculty who are not graduate students and whose activity report indicates teaching and research are to generate research space. It should be recognized that the basis for employment may vary from the activity in which they are engaged. Also, it should be repeated that those graduate students who are registered on an in absentia basis and those graduate students who have not declared a major department should not generate space. Institutional policy should determine if those graduate students registered for "no credit" enrollment should generate research space. It is recommended that they do not.

To account for the variations in the space requirement of a given field of study, a concept called the "research demand factor" has been developed. This value is to be multiplied by the total research demand units for a field of study to get the total amount of research space generated for that given department. The following research demand factors (RDF) are recommended:

Department	Recommended Research Demand Factors
Agriculture	
Agriculture Economics	1.0
Agriculture Engineering	45.0
Agronomy	26.0
Animal Science	28.0
Dairy Science	28.0
Food Science	28.0
Forestry	30.0
Home Economics	30.0
Horticulture	28.0
Plant Pathology	26.0
Commerce	
Accountancy	0.5
Business Education	0.5
Economics	0.5
Finance	0.5
Business Administration	1.0
Industrial Administration	5.0
Marketing	0.5
Bureau of Economics and Business Research	0.5
Bureau of Business Management	0.5
Business English	0.5
Education	
Education Administration and Supervision	0.5
Educational Psychology	2.0
Elementary Education	0.5
History and Philosophy of Education	0.5
Secondary and Continuing Education	0.5
Vocational and Technical Education	10.0
Bureau of Educational Research	10.0
Center for Instructional Research and Curriculm Evaluation	5.0
Institute of Research on Exceptional Children	6.0
Student Teaching	0.5
Engineering	
Aeronautical and Astronautical Engineering	30.0
Ceramic Engineering	30.0

Department	Recommended Research Demand Factors
Civil Engineering	30.0
Electrical Engineering	25.0
General Engineering	25.0
Materials Research	25.0
Measurement Program	25.0
Mechanical Engineering	25.0
Industrial Engineering	25.0
Mining Engineering	25.0
Metallurgy Engineering	25.0
Petroleum Engineering	25.0
Nuclear Engineering	25.0
Physics	25.0
Theoretical and Applied Mechanics	30.0
Fine and Applied Arts	
Architecture	20.0
Art	35.0
Band	0.5
Bureau of Community Planning	20.0
Landscape Architecture	20.0
Music	0.5
Theater	15.0
Urban Planning	20.0
Graduate College	
Computer Science	10.0
Physical Environment Unit	25.0
Radiocarbon Lab	25.0
Journalism	
Advertising	1.0
Journalism	1.0
Radio and TV	1.0
Institute of Communications	1.0
National Association of Educational Broadcasters	0.0
Broadcasting and Radio	10.0
TV and Motion Pictures	25.0
Liberal Arts and Sciences	
Anthropology	7.5
Asian Area Studies	0.5
Astronomy	7.5
Botany	25.0
Chemistry	25.0
Classics	0.5
English	0.5
Entomology	25.0
French	0.5
Division of General Studies	5.0
Geography	5.0
Geology	25.0
German	0.5
History	0.5
Latin American Studies	0.5
Life Sciences	25.0
Linguistics	0.5
Mathematics	0.5
Microbiology	25.0
Philosophy	0.5
Physics	25.0
Physiology	25.0

Department	Recommended Research Demand Factors
Political Science	0.5
Psychology	15.0
Russian	0.5
Sociology	2.0
Spanish	0.5
Speech	8.3
Zoology	25.0
Physical Education	
Physical Education for Men	5.0
Physical Education for Women	7.5
Recreation	7.5
Health and Safety	15.0
Intramural	0.0
Rehabilitation Center	7.5
Armed Forces	
Air Force Science	0.5
Military Science	0.5
Naval Science	0.5
Other	
Government and Public Affairs	5.0
Labor Relations	5.0
Social Work	1.5
Library Science	0.5

ARCHIVE AND RESEARCH EQUIPMENT STORAGE

Most departments require some space to store seldom-used records and various types of research equipment not in current use. This "building block" of space is required for inactive records that cannot be destroyed and various types of research equipment that is too valuable to be discarded. On most campuses, this type of space is usually found in portions of the basements and attics. It is recommended that future development of this type of space be accommodated in relatively low-cost buildings.

To account for this type of space, it is recommended that a certain percentage of the total departmental space (instructional laboratory, office, and research) be calculated to generate this space requirement. It should be stated that the space requirement, and in turn the space generated, is above and beyond the active records space in office areas and active equipment space connected to the instructional and research laboratories. These active storage space requirements are considered as auxiliary areas to the prime function of space, and are included in their respective space standards.

The following are the recommended percentages to be used for archive and research equipment storage:

Field of Study	Per Cent
Administration	
Secretary to the Board (25 per cent if academic personnel records are in this office)	10
President's Office	10
Administrative Vice-President	10

Field of Study	Per Cent
Academic Vice-President	10
Business Vice-President	10
Bureau of Institutional Research	10
Space Office	10
Student Counseling	10
Data Processing	25
Insurance Office	10
Business Office	10
Purchasing	10
Military Property Custodian	10
Admissions and Records	10
Legal Counsel	10
Nonacademic Personnel	10
Public Information Office	10
Photographic Laboratory	20
Dean of Students	10
Dean of Men	10
Dean of Women	10
Placement Office	10
Security Office	10
Alumni Relations and Records	10
Retirement Office	10
Architect's Office	10
University Honors Program	10
Agriculture	
Agriculture Administration	10
Agriculture Economics	1
Agriculture Engineering	20
Agronomy	10
Animal Science	2
Dairy Science	2
Food Science	2
Forestry	5
Home Economics	2
Horticulture	5
Plant Pathology	5
Vocational Agriculture	1
Commerce	
Commerce Administration	10
Accountancy	1
Business Education	1
Economics	1
Finance	1
Business Administration	1
Industrial Administration	1
Marketing	1
Bureau of Economics and Business Research	1
Bureau of Business Management	1
Business English	1
Education	
Education Administration	10
Education Administration and Supervision	1
Educational Psychology	1
Elementary Education	1
History and Philosophy of Education	1
Secondary and Continuing Education	1
Vocational and Technical Education	2

Field of Study	Per Cent
Bureau of Educational Research	1
Center for Instructional Research and Curriculum Evaluation	1
Institute of Research on Exceptional Children	1
Student Teaching	1
Engineering	
Engineering Administration	10
Aeronautical and Astronautical Engineering	5
Ceramic Engineering	5
Civil Engineering	5
Electrical Engineering	5
General Engineering	2
Materials Research	2
Measurement Program	2
Mechanical Engineering	5
Industrial Engineering	5
Mining Engineering	5
Metallurgy Engineering	5
Petroleum Engineering	5
Nuclear Engineering	5
Physics	5
Theoretical and Applied Mechanics	5
Fine and Applied Arts	
Fine and Applied Arts Administration	10
Architecture	1
Art	1
Band	2
Bureau of Community Planning	1
Landscape Architecture	1
Music	2
Theater	10
Urban Planning	1
Graduate College	
Graduate College Administration	10
Computer Science	5
Physical Environment Unit	1
Radiocarbon Lab	1
Journalism	
Journalism Administration	10
Advertising	1
Journalism	1
Radio and TV	1
Institute of Communications	2
Broadcasting and Radio	2
TV and Motion Pictures	2
Liberal Arts and Sciences	
Liberal Arts and Sciences Administration	10
Anthropology	5
Asian Area Studies	1
Astronomy	1
Botany	5
Chemistry	5
Classics	1
English	1
Entomology	5

Field of Study	Per Cent
French	1
Division of General Studies	1
Geography	1
Geology	5
German	1
History	1
Latin American Studies	1
Life Sciences	5
Linguistics	1
Mathematics	1
Microbiology	5
Physics	5
Philosophy	1
Physiology	5
Political Science	1
Psychology	3
Russian	1
Sociology	1
Spanish	1
Speech	1
Zoology	5
Physical Education	
Physical Education Administration	10
Physical Education for Men	1
Physical Education for Women	1
Recreation	1
Health and Safety	1
Intramural	1
Armed Forces	
Air Force Science	1
Military Science	1
Naval Science	1
Other	
Government and Public Affairs	1
Labor Relations	1
Social Work	1
Library Science	1

LIBRARY SPACE

Library space is that space used for the collection, storage, circulation, and use of books, periodicals, manuscripts, and other reading materials. The library "building block" can be further broken down into three subdivisions — stack space, reader space, and service space.

The stack or collection space is based on the number of volumes and periodicals to be catalogued. The space required is usually planned so that each shelf is filled to about 75 per cent of capacity. This is to prevent the unnecessary movements of books as the total collection increases. Under these conditions, the space for the stack collections is 0.1 square foot per bound volume; or it takes one square foot for ten bound volumes. However, as the total collection increases, the need for aisles and access space in the stack area decreases, and the shelves holding some of the least used books can be filled to a greater capacity. The recommended standards for stack or collection space are shown below:

First 150,000 volumes	.1 NASF per bound volume
Second 150,000 volumes	.09 NASF per bound volume
Next 300,000 volumes	.08 NASF per bound volume
All volumes in excess of 600,000 volumes	.07 NASF per bound volume

There are certain materials other than books stored in libraries that require stack space. It is recommended that space be provided for these materials on a conversion basis as shown below:

Type of Material	Unit	Conversion Ratio Unit to Volume
Roughly Classified Pamphlets	Item[a]	15 to 1
Music Scores and Parts	Item	15 to 1
Sound Recordings	Record	6 to 1
Microfilm Reels	Reel	4 to 1
Maps	Map	9 to 1
Archival Materials	Cubic Feet	1 to 15

[a] A pamphlet, score, or one grouping in a manila folder equals one item. A grouping in a manila folder may consist of one paper or related papers.

Again, it should be pointed out that the stack space requirement should only include those bound volumes and materials that are housed in space under the control of the library administration. It should not include those departmental or individual collections housed in the office or conference areas of the individual or department.

Reading areas in many libraries have been based upon the total enrollment. In many cases, the standards have been 30 square feet per reading station with a station capacity for 25 per cent of the student body. These standards are believed to be adequate for undergraduate reading room space; but as the graduate program of an institution increases, there is a need for carrel space for both graduate students and faculty. The demand for carrel space varies by field of study. Those fields of study that do not require laboratory research space will require more carrel space for both graduate students and faculty. Based on these premises, the following standards are recommended for reading room space:

1. 7.5 square feet per FTE undergraduate student.
2. 7.5 square feet per headcount beginning graduate student.
3. 7.5 square feet per headcount advanced graduate student in those fields of study with high research requirement (those fields of study that have a research demand factor greater than one).
4. 15 square feet per headcount advanced graduate student in those fields of study with low research requirements (those fields of study that have a research demand factor of one or less).
5. 15 square feet per FTE teaching and research faculty (with the rank of instructor or above) in those departments that have low research requirements (those departments with a research demand factor of one or less).

6. 3 square feet per FTE teaching and research faculty (with rank of instructor or above) in those departments that have high research requirements (those departments with a research demand factor of greater than one).

Those faculty engaged in activities such as administration and counseling do not generate library reading space, nor does any nonacademic employee.

Library service space includes both technical service and public service areas. It is to include the office and workroom areas necessary for the administration, acquisition, and cataloging of all volumes. It is recommended that the determination of this type of space be based on a percentage of reader space with 25 per cent being the value used. Where branch libraries are to be constructed, only 20 per cent of the reader space should be allowed for service space within the branch library, the remaining five percent to be allowed in the main library. The five per cent maintained in the main library is to accommodate the activities connected with centralized acquisition and cataloging.

COMMONS SPACE

In addition to the facilities in the union building, there should be lounge space provided in academic buildings. These lounges are to provide space for those students who are between scheduled classes and do not have time to return to their residence halls. It is recommended that one and one-half square feet per FTE student be provided for this type of space. In institutions with many commuters, an additional one square foot per FTE student is required to provide locker space for books and class materials brought to the campus by students. The commuter students, unlike the students on a residential campus, do not have the opportunity to return to the residence halls to leave off and pick up additional books. This locker space is provided because it is not reasonable to expect a student to carry the class materials needed for one day to all classes.

PHYSICAL PLANT SPACE

Physical facilities for the physical plant department fall into two categories — office space and maintenance space. The space standard for offices (135 NASF per FTE) should be used for all operational and maintenance personnel who require office space. The maintenance space for shops, material storage, etc. should be determined on the basis of the number of net assignable square feet to be served. A value of 2.2 per cent of the net assignable square feet to be served is recommended for the determination of the amount of maintenance space needed. The 2.2 per cent standard for maintenance space will not allow a small college to have all the various kinds of shops that a large university will have; however, as a college grows larger, the director of the physical plant will have to decide which functions his organization should perform and which functions should be bid to outside firms.

In projecting physical plant space, it may be necessary to exclude certain net assignable square feet on campus because this space is serviced and maintained by other than the physical plant personnel. A good example of this type of space is the residence halls on a campus where the maintenance and operation of these student housing and food service facilities are provided by their own personnel. The total maintenance space required for any campus is to be derived by adding the projected NASF to the existing NASF to be served by the physical plant department, times the value of 2.2 per cent.

When projecting the total office requirement for the physical plant, a ratio of the net assignable square feet served per person requiring office space is obtained from the existing conditions and used for the projected years. An example of a physical plant department calculation is as follows:

Total NASF on campus	6,000,000
Less: Space not served by the physical plant	2,000,000
Total NASF served by the physical plant department	4,000,000
Total NASF of maintenance space (2.2 per cent of 4,000,000)	88,000
Total number of physical plant personnel requiring office space	150
Total NASF of office space required (150 × 135)	20,250
Total NASF of physical plant department space required (88,000 + 20,250)	108,250

On the basis of this example, personnel requiring office space would be projected at the ratio of 1 per 26,667 NASF (4,000,000 ÷ 150).

STUDENT SERVICES

Included in the student services "building block" are those facilities that one would normally associate with the student union building. It includes meeting rooms; lounge areas; dining areas; game rooms such as billiards, bowling and table tennis; bookstore areas; guest rooms; and the office and workroom space for the administration of these services. Included are the office and work areas for all student activity organizations. For a residential type of institution, it is recommended that 8.25 net assignable square feet be provided for each FTE student. In commuter-type institutions, an additional one NASF per FTE student should be provided for additional lounge and vending facilities. It is suggested that the additional lounge and vending facilities be located in sub-centers if the campus is spread out over a large area; if not, these facilities should be located within the union building complex.

HEALTH SERVICE

The "building block" of health service encompasses all facilities normally associated with the campus health service unit. It includes such areas as examination rooms, treatment rooms, observation wards, laboratories, office space for physicians and supporting staff, reception-waiting areas, supply rooms, and infirmary facilities. Infirmary facilities include space for resident physicians and nurses, private rooms, general wards, and food preparation for patients and staff.

The type of health service facilities required is usually a matter of institutional policy. In general, the types and quantities of facilities needed falls into two categories — nonresidential universities not requiring infirmary facilities, and residential universities requiring infirmary facilities. For analysis and projection of this category, physical facilities should be based on the number of people to be served; therefore, the total FTE students should form the basis. The following standards are recommended:

Net Assignable Square Feet per FTE Student

FTE Students	Residential Universities with Infirmary Facilities	Nonresidential Universities Without Infirmary Facilities
First 2,000	4.0	1.0
Next 3,000	3.0	0.9
Second 5,000	2.5	0.8
Third 5,000	2.0	0.7
Beyond 15,000	1.5	0.6

The above building space requirements were developed and published by the California State Department of Education (*A Restudy of the Needs of California in Higher Eduction,* Sacramento, 1955), and appear to be the most realistic indices available for study of these physical facilities requirements.

INACTIVE SPACE

Every campus has, at any one point in time, some space in the process of being remodeled. This remodeling has been caused by a reassignment of space or an upgrading of space in older buildings to meet the present-day needs for instruction and research. On a campus where the majority of the buildings are 50 or 60 years old, the area unassigned because of remodeling may be substantial. On a relatively new campus, this area may not be significant; therefore, on a campus with a mixture of old and new buildings, it is recommended that one per cent of the total academic space be generated to account for the space that cannot be used for academic pursuits because of remodeling.

AUDITORIUM AND MUSEUM SPACE NOT FOR INSTRUCTION OR RESEARCH

Every college or university has auditoriums and museums that are not directly related to the regular instruction and research programs. These areas are primarily used for public service programs. The total space required for both these types of areas is a matter of institutional policy, and will vary substantially from one institution to another, depending upon the role assumed by the university; therefore, no space standard is proposed.

GYMNASIUM SPACE NOT FOR INSTRUCTION

Although gymnasiums are treated under instructional laboratories, they actually serve more than one function in an institution. In addition to fulfilling the instructional laboratory requirements, they may also serve as recreational facilities for the students, faculty, and staff and as facilities for the varsity athletic program.

The method of calculating the instructional gymnasiums was presented in the foregoing section; therefore, no further elaboration is needed here. The level and degree of involvement in the varsity athletic program is a matter of policy; therefore, no attempt will be made to propose standards for projecting or analyzing the activity areas, locker and shower areas, or seating requirements for this particular program.

The physical facility requirements for the recreational needs of an institution need to be analyzed to determine if sufficient facilities are generated by the instructional gymnasium standards. Generally, the recreational requirements will be met by the instructional gymnasium standards for a commuter institution. However, in a residential institution, specific requirements for recreation must be met. A calculation of physical facilities should be made to determine the need both from the viewpoint of instructional requirements and recreational requirements. The larger of the two requirements should be used in determining the total physical education space needed. It is proposed that the recreational requirements of a residential institution be based on the following:

1. Nine NASF of indoor activity area is needed for each undergraduate student.

2. Space requirements for lockers, showers, drying, storage, and supply areas should equal 35 per cent of the activity space. Therefore, each undergraduate student should require 12.1 NASF of physical education space ($9 \times 1.35 = 12.1$).

3. Graduate students participate in sports and physical recreation 25 per cent as extensively as undergraduates. Therefore, the physical education facilities for recreation generated by graduate students equals headcount graduate students times .25 times 12.1.

4. Fifteen per cent of the staff (academic and nonacademic) makes use of physical education facilities for recreation. Therefore, the physical education facilities for recreation generated by the staff equals headcount staff times .15 times 12.1.

Those physical facilities needed for the various intercollegiate athletic programs may have to be added to the recommended standard for instructional gymnasiums and for recreational space. The additional space required varies with the extent to which an institution is involved in varsity athletics. The institution may or may not need to add additional activity areas to the standard recommended above, depending on whether or not scheduling permits the use of the space for instruction, recreation, and varsity athletics. Additional auxiliary space for showers, lockers, and equipment storage for personnel in varsity athletics must be provided in addition to those standards recommended, as they are separate from the instruction and recreation auxiliary areas.

Spectator seating adjacent to all activity areas must be in addition to the recommended standards. Because of the wide variation in institutional policies regarding athletic programs, no attempt will be made to analyze or project this type of space.

MISCELLANEOUS

Purchasing Stores. Most universities have receiving and warehouse facilities to store office supplies, office furniture, laboratory supplies, and volatile and nonvolatile chemicals. Whether or not this activity is centralized, the total space requirements do not change. If it is centralized, the space generated is assigned to that organizational unit. If this activity is decentralized, the space generated must be allocated to the various units assigned, based on distribution of activities. The space required for this activity is related to the number and level of student to be served. The recommended space indices are as follows:

Level of Student	Net Assignable Square Feet per FTE Student
Lower Division	1.0
Upper Division	1.5
Beginning Graduates	2.0
Advanced Graduates	4.5

R.O.T.C. Uniform Storage. At universities where there are Reserve Officer Training Corps programs, there exists a requirement for uniform and supply storage. It is recommended that the space requirement for this activity be 12 net assignable square feet per FTE student enrolled in any of the military programs.

THE "NUMERIC METHOD" APPLIED TO THE EDUCATIONAL PROGRAMS IN LAW AND VETERINARY MEDICINE

At this time, the "Numeric Method" of calculating physical facility requirements has been developed for only two professional programs — law and veterinary medicine. It is hoped that in the future the "Numeric Method" can be applied to the educational programs in medicine, dentistry, nursing, and pharmacy. The professional programs are more varied and special space requirements are needed; therefore a separate discussion of the law and veterinary medicine programs will follow.

LAW

The majority of educational programs in law are located in a building used exclusively for law and with the facilities seldom shared with other units. Also, in the case of most professional programs, the student spends most of the day in these academic facilities. If he is not in class then he is in the library or a lounge. The physical facility requirements of the College of Law can be categorized into "building blocks," but because of some special requirements the standards vary from those given previously. The following are the recommended space standards for the educational program in law.

Classrooms

Because of the large number of books used in the classes by students in the College of Law, most law classrooms are furnished with tables and chairs. This results in an increased station size from 15 square feet to 16.5 square feet, and the resulting classroom standard recommended is .92 square feet per weekly student hour.

Instructional Laboratories

No instructional laboratories are required. If in the future the educational program should require laboratory space, an evaluation of the activities conducted would have to be made and then a standard developed.

Office Space

It is recommended that the normal office standard of 135 square feet per FTE for those requiring office space be maintained for this program. In most cases the faculty members in the College of Law do their research in the office and as such require additional storage space for books and writing. In many cases when planning new facilities it may be desirable to incorporate the research space generated with the office space to provide a somewhat larger private office.

Research Space

The faculty and graduate students (those working for a degree above the first professional degree) will generate research space. Those students working for their first professional degree in law will not generate research space. The following research demand units are recommended:

FTE Research Faculty	15 RDU
FTE Teaching Faculty	3 RDU
Headcount Graduate Student	15 RDU

The research demand factor (RDF) recommended is 15. Therefore, the research space required can be obtained by multiplying the total RDU times the RDF. When the research space is planned in a building, some of the space is usually combined with the office space to provide the additional space required for the individual library of each law faculty member and the remainder is usually planned in conference rooms that are used for meetings between the graduate students and the faculty.

Archive and Research Equipment Storage

It is recommended that one per cent of the total office and research space be provided for storage space.

Library Space

The library for the College of Law is usually located within the law facilities. The generation of law library space is based upon the same method as outlined in Chapter 5, i.e., the generation of stack space, reader space, and service space. Studies have indicated the average size of the volumes in law libraries is larger than in the usual college library. To make adjustments for this additional stack requirement, the following stack standards are recommended for law libraries:

First 150,000 volumes	.18 NASF per bound volume
Second 150,000 volumes	.16 NASF per bound volume
Next 300,000 volumes	.14 NASF per bound volume
All volumes in excess of 600,000	.13 NASF per bound volume

Studies of library occupancy indicate that law students spend more time in library facilities than students in other colleges. This will make the reading space requirements substantially higher than those recommended for the library standard in Chapter 5. It is recommended that reader space in the College of Law be provided on the basis of seating 50 per cent of the students at 30 square feet per station. This results in a standard of 15 square feet per FTE student.

The service space standard for the law library should be the same as that recommended in Chapter 5. If the law library personnel handle their own book acquisitions, 25 per cent of the reading space should be allowed for service space. However, if the law library works through the central library on book acquisitions, 20 per cent of the reading space should be allowed in the law library for service space and the remaining 5 per cent should be allocated to the central library for book acquisitions.

Commons Space

The commons space provided for College of Law students will be influenced by the proximity of housing space for law students. In some institutions residential space for law students is provided in adjacent facilities; thus, some of the commons space is provided as residential space. In those cases where residential space is not provided adjacent to the academic facilities it is recommended that lounge and locker areas be provided. It is recommended that 2.5 square feet per FTE student be provided for lounge space. This is the same standard as used for commuter institutions where the student comes in the morning and spends all day in the academic facilities. Since many law students require a typewriter and since, as previously mentioned, the books are quite large, it is recommended that each FTE student be provided a full-length locker. This will require approximately 4.75 square feet per FTE student.

Law Forum Space

When there is a student publication in the school of law, space must be provided for this activity. It is recommended that two square feet per professional student be provided to generate the necessary office and workroom space.

Courtroom Space

It is highly desirable to provide courtroom space for the law program. If a courtroom is to be provided, 12 square feet per person to be seated is recommended to provide for spectator seating, judges, jury, and legal counsels.

VETERINARY MEDICINE

The educational programs in veterinary medicine are usually conducted in buildings exclusively for students in this field of study. The facilities required for this program are very similar to those required for the biological sciences, with the exception that animal quarters are required in conjunction with the instructional laboratories, research laboratories, and clinic facilities. Also, unlike most facilities discussed in the previous chapter, some of the physical facilities required may be planned in farm structures.

Classrooms

Since the facilities for a veterinary medicine college are usually located on the perimeter of a campus, classrooms will not be available to other academic units due to the distance factor. This will, in all probability, result in lower utilization. Assuming the hours per week to be scheduled will be ten per cent below that of general university classrooms, a standard of .92 NASF per weekly student hour is recommended for classroom facilities of the veterinary medicine program, if the general university classroom standard is .833 NASF per weekly student hour.

Office Space

It is recommended that the normal office standard of 135 NASF per FTE for those requiring office space be used for the veterinary medicine program.

Instructional Laboratory Space

The laboratory facility requirements for the basic science instructional programs of the College of Veterinary Medicine are quite similar to those in the biological science program. Therefore, a student station size of 68 square feet including auxiliary facilities is recommended. This station size will result in a requirement of 4.25 square feet per laboratory contact hour if the laboratories are utilized 20 hours per week with an 80 per cent student station utilization, or 3.54 square feet per laboratory contact hour if the laboratories are scheduled 24 hours per week with an 80 per cent student station utilization.

Research Laboratory Space

The research laboratory facilities for veterinary medicine are very much like those in the biological sciences. However, the research efforts of graduate students and faculty are divided between laboratory activities and animal research investigation. The space for the animal research investigation will be provided as animal quarter space and will be discussed later in this chapter. For the research laboratory space it is recommended that a research demand factor (RDF) of 15 be used for veterinary medicine. The professional students (DVM candidates) have very little time outside of scheduled laboratory and clinic requirements to do research, thus they should not generate research space. The faculty and the graduate students (post-DVM candidates) will generate research space in the same manner as outlined in Chapter 5. The following is a summary of the research demand units and the research demand factors recommended for research laboratory facilities in the veterinary medicine program:

FTE Teaching Faculty	3 RDU	15 RDF
FTE Research Faculty	15 RDU	15 RDF
Headcount Graduate Student	15 RDU	15 RDF

Commons Space

The veterinary medicine student usually spends all day in the veterinary medicine facilities; therefore, commons facilities should be provided on the basis of 2.5 square feet per FTE student.

Locker and Cleanup Space

Because the students in veterinary medicine will be required to make a complete change of clothes for some of the clinical and laboratory activities, lockers, showers, and those restrooms adjacent to locker-shower facilities should be provided for all students and most staff. The following standard is recommended for those students and FTE staff requiring locker and cleanup space:

Locker space	8.5 NASF per person
Cleanup space	1.5 NASF per person
Total	10.0 NASF per person

Library Space

As in the case of the College of Law, a library for veterinary medicine is usually included as part of the veterinary medicine building complex. The requirements for reader space are the same as those outlined in Chapter 5. However, the average size of the volumes in the field of veterinary medicine is larger than those normally contained in the general library. To allow for the larger volume size, the recommended stack standards are the same as for the College of Law (see p. 73).

The service space standard for a veterinary medicine library should be the same as that recommended in Chapter 5. If the veterinary medicine library personnel handle their own book acquisitions, 25 per cent of the reading space should be allowed for service space. However, if the veterinary medicine library works through the central library on book acquisitions, 20 per cent of the reading space should be allowed in the veterinary medicine library for service space and the remaining 5 per cent should be allocated to the central library for book acquisitions.

Animal Quarters Space

As indicated above, the space requirements to house animals was not discussed in the previous chapters because it was assumed that the small number of animals needed in conjunction with the instructional and research laboratories would be accommodated within the recommended space standards. However, the veterinary medicine educational program requires a substantial number of large animals, and specific space allowances must be made for this activity. Animal quarters space is required for those animals used by the professional (DVM) students in the instructional laboratories and clinical facilities, and by the graduate students and faculty in the research laboratories. The total amount of animal quarters space needed for any school or college of veterinary medicine will depend upon the type and quantity of animals used in their specific educational programs. For the most part, faculty and graduate student preferences and interests for specific types of animals will govern, to a large extent, the total space required. When the type and number of animals are determined, the following areas per type of animal are recommended:

Type of Animal	Net Assignable Square Foot per Animal
Mice	.5
Rats, guinea pigs, gerbils	1.0
Rabbits, cats, chickens	4.0
Dogs, including run area	30.0
Calves, sheep, pigs	24.0
Hogs, tie stall for cattle or horse	48.0
Cattle or horse stall	144.0

The above areas include circulation around the cages and pens in a room, but do not include aisles in the large animal stall areas as these are not considered net assignable square feet. The above areas per type of animal are the basis for the following discussion on animal quarters requirements.

Because the type and quantity of animals will vary substantially from one institution to another, no attempt will be made to recommend specific animal quarters standards. Rather, a discussion centered around the manner in which the space office at the University of Illinois determines the total requirements will be presented. It is hoped this discussion will enable other institutions to assess their space requirements for animal quarters. It should be noted that the values stated in the following discussion were determined in cooperation with the faculty of the College of Veterinary Medicine at the University of Illinois and are representative of space requirements for this specific educational program.

Before proceeding with a discussion of specific animal quarters requirements, the basis for stating these requirements must be clearly understood. Space requirements may be stated in terms of the entering student or the total students enrolled. If the space requirements are stated in terms of the entering class, then the requirements for all four years of the program must be totaled for each department in the college and divided by the entering class size. If the requirements are stated in terms of total students enrolled, then the requirements for all four years must be totaled for all departments in the college and divided by the total number of students enrolled in all four years. When looking into the future, enrollment projections will probably be made on an entering class basis. To project the total enrollment, a student retention rate must be determined. For planning purposes at the University of Illinois, the following retention rates are used for the College of Veterinary Medicine: first year, 100 per cent; second year, 92 per cent; third year, 90 per cent; fourth year, 90 per cent. Therefore, if an institution had an entering class size of 100 students, the total enrollment would be 372 (100 + 92 + 90 + 90 = 372). This retention rate must be determined before the future space requirements per student can be assessed.

Instructional Animal Quarters

Instructional animal quarters are required to house those animals that are to be used in the instructional laboratories. Most of the space implications for this activity are in the first two years of the program. At the University of Illinois the total quantity of animal quarters space related to the institutional laboratories is 16 net assignable square feet per student enrolled or 5,952 (16 ×372) total net assignable square feet for 100 entering students. Also, this can be expressed as 59.52 NASF per entering student. Figure 9 indicates the format to be used in assessing the instructional animal quarters requirements for a particular institution.

Figure 9. Format for Determining Instructional Animal Quarters Requirements

Column 1	Column 2	Column 3	Column 4	Column 5	Column 6
Department	Type of Animal	NASF per Animal	Prof. Students per Animal	NASF per Prof. Student	Total NASF by Department

An explanation of Figure 9 follows:

Column 1. Listed here should be the department that requires instructional animal quarters space, e.g., Physiology, Pharmacology, Pathology, etc.

Column 2. Indicate the type of animals required.

Column 3. Enter the net assignable square feet required per type of animal as indicated earlier in this discussion.

Column 4. Enter the number of students per type of animal indicated in Column 3.

Column 5. Enter the net assignable square feet required per professional student by dividing Column 3 by Column 4, e.g. one dog (at 30 NASF) per four students (30 ÷ 4) = 7.50. Another example is: one horse (at 144 NASF) per 20 students (144 ÷ 20) = 7.20.

Column 6. Enter the total NASF from Column 4 for each department. The total of Column 6 will result in the number of net assignable square feet needed per student for instructional animal quarters requirements.

Clinic Facilities

The total amount of clinic facilities, like instructional animal quarters, depends on the type and quantity of animals required in a specific educational program. For this reason no attempt will be made to recommend standards for clinic facilities. The following discussion represents the basis on which the University of Illinois is planning and projecting clinic facilities. The values indicated may vary from one institution to another depending upon the specific educational program.

It is recognized that clinic facilities are used mostly by fourth-year students and on a limited basis by third-year students. Therefore, it was concluded that the clinic facilities should be stated in terms of the fourth-year professional student. Further analysis indicates that clinic facilities fall into three categories — small animal, large animal, and general clinic facilities. The following represent the space guidelines used for projecting facilities at the University of Illinois for each of the three clinic categories:

Small Animal Clinic Space

Activity	Net Assignable Square Feet per Fourth-Year Professional Student
Animal Quarters	105
Dogs and cats are the most common animals housed. The space required should be equal to three and one-half dogs per student (30 × 3.5 = 105)	
Examination Area	11
Treatment Area	21
Surgery and Recovery Area	25
Clinic Auxiliary Area	30
This area includes food storage and preparation, instrument storage, sterilization, cart storage, etc.	
Waiting and Reception	10
Total NASF	202

Large Animal Clinic Space

Activity	Net Assignable Square Feet per Fourth-Year Professional Student
Animal Quarters	252
One and three-fourths stalls per student (144 × 1.75 = 252)	
Exercise Area	26
Treatment Area	50
Surgery and Recovery Area	28
Clinic Auxiliary Area	25
Feed, Hay, and Bedding Storage	85
Waiting and Reception	10
Total NASF	476

General Clinic Facilities

ACTIVITY	NET ASSIGNABLE SQUARE FEET PER FOURTH-YEAR PROFESSIONAL STUDENT
Pharmacy Area	44
Radiology Area	34
Pathology Area	12
Resident Student Caretakers Area (dormitory and dining areas)	14
Total NASF	104

Summary of Clinic Facilities

CATEGORY	NET ASSIGNABLE SQUARE FEET PER FOURTH-YEAR PROFESSIONAL STUDENT
Small Animal	202
Large Animal	476
General Clinic Facilities	104
Total NASF	782

To convert the NASF per fourth-year professional student to other bases, the enrollment retention rate must be used. The comparable value based upon total enrollment is 189 $\left[782 \times \frac{90 \text{ (4th yr)}}{372 \text{ (total)}} \right]$, and the value based upon the entering class is 704 $\left[782 \times \frac{90 \text{ (4th yr)}}{100 \text{ (entering)}} \right]$.

Graduate Student and Faculty Animal Quarters Space

The type and quantity of animals used in research by graduate students and faculty vary widely from one institution to another. In fact, there is a substantial variation from one research person to another. It is also recognized that some graduate students and faculty do not use any animals in their research projects. Therefore, like instructional animal quarters and clinic facilities, no specific standards will be recommended. The following indicates the values used for this activity at the University of Illinois:

Headcount Graduate Student	315 NASF
FTE Teaching Faculty	40 NASF
FTE Research Faculty	240 NASF

Figure 9 above indicates the format used in tabulating these values. It must be realized that the above values are averages for the total graduate students enrolled or faculty employed. It represents values for projection purposes only. It does not indicate how the space should be assigned once it is constructed. This matter should be left to the judgment of the college or school administration. The institution must also decide what portion of the animal quarters space must be accommodated in permanent buildings versus farm structures. Again, many factors enter into this decision; therefore, each institution must decide this for itself. At the University of Illinois planning is based upon 75 per cent of the animal quarters requirements for graduate students and faculty being planned in permanent buildings with 25 per cent planned in farm structures.

Storage

Storage facility requirements for veterinary medicine are quite varied. Storage facilities must include provisions for inactive records, research equipment not in use, and hay and feed for animals. It is recommended that the storage factor be 20 per cent of the NASF generated for office, instructional laboratory, instructional animal quarters, research laboratory, and animal quarters for graduate students and faculty. Of this, at least one-half of the storage should be planned in farm structures for hay, feed, and bedding materials. It should be noted that the storage factor of 20 per cent should not be applied to the clinic facilities because storage allowances are included in the clinic space guidelines.

AN ILLUSTRATION OF THE SPACE CALCULATIONS FOR A HYPOTHETICAL COLLEGE OF VETERINARY MEDICINE

The following is an illustration of the space calculations for a hypothetical College of Veterinary Medicine. It is hoped that the foregoing discussion will become clearer as a result of showing the data necessary for calculating the space requirements and the actual space calculations for a hypothetical college.

Institutional Data Necessary for Calculating Space Requirements

ENROLLMENT		FTE Requiring Office Space	218.50
Professional (DVM)		FTE Requiring Locker Space	178.00[a]
First Year	100	Classroom — Weekly Student	
Second Year	92	Hours	4,246
Third Year	90	Laboratory — Weekly Student	
Fourth Year	90	Hours	6,871
Total Professional	372	Volumes in the Library	45,000
Graduate Students		(book acquisition through	
FTE	61	central library)	
Headcount	117		
FTE Faculty			
Teaching	40.02		
Research	56.54		
Other (Administration,			
Counseling, etc.)	15.72		

[a] Academic and nonacademic staff.

Space Calculations

	NASF
Office Space (135 × 218.50)	29,498
Instructional Space	
Laboratories (6,871 × 4.25)	29,202
Animal Quarters (16 × 372)	5,952

Space Calculations — (Continued)

		NASF
Research Space		
Laboratories		
Graduate Students (15 × 15 × 117)	26,325	
FTE Teaching Faculty (3 × 15 × 40.02)	1,801	
FTE Research Faculty (15 × 15 × 56.54)	12,722	
Total Research Laboratory Space		40,848
Animal Quarters		
Graduate Students (315 × 117)	36,855	
FTE Teaching Faculty (40 × 40.02)	1,601	
FTE Research Faculty (240 × 56.54)	13,570	
Total Research Animal Quarters Space		52,026
Subtotal		157,526
Storage (.20 × 157,526)		31,505
Commons (372 + 61) × 2.5		1,083
Locker and Cleanup Space		
Students (372 + 117) × 10	4,890	
Staff (178 × 10)	1,780	
Total Locker and Cleanup Space		6,670
Clinic Facilities (189 × 372)		70,308
Classroom Space (4,246 × .92)		3,906
Library Space		
Stack Space (45,000 × .18)		8,100
Reader Space		
DVM Students (372 × 7.5)	2,790	
Graduate Students (117 × 7.5)	878	
Teaching Faculty (40.02 × 3)	120	
Research Faculty (56.54 × 3)	170	
Total Reader Space		3,958
Service Space at Veterinary Medicine Library		792
Service Space at Main Library		198
Total Library Space		13,048
Total NASF for a hypothetical College of Veterinary Medicine		284,046

Of the above facilities, the following would be planned in farm structures:

    Animal quarters for graduate students
        and faculty (.25 × 52,026)   13,007 NASF
        Storage (.50 × 31,505)   15,753 NASF
        Total NASF   28,760 NASF

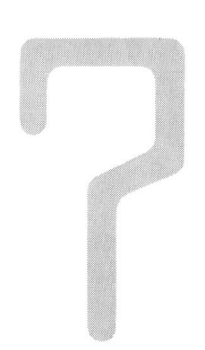

SUMMARIZATION AND PRESENTATION OF PHYSICAL FACILITY DATA

Chapter 4 outlined the institutional data needed for proper analysis and Chapter 5 provided a method and indices with which to project physical facilities. To provide a clearer understanding of the material presented in those chapters, an example of the data required and the calculation procedures for the projection of space required for a hypothetical Chemistry Department is given below. Line numbers are given to provide ease in describing the operations performed.

Line No.		Base Year	Projected Year 19XX
1	Freshman-Sophomore FTE	(120)	(130)
2	Junior-Senior FTE	(160)	(200)
3	Prof. and Beg. Grad. FTE	(40)	(50)
4	Advanced Grad. FTE	(30)	(50)
5	Total FTE Students	(350)	(430)
6	Headcount Beg. Grad.	(52)	(66)
7	Headcount Advanced Grad.	(40)	(66)
8	Weekly Student Hours in Classroom	(1000)	(1400)
9	Weekly Student Hours in Laboratory	(1200)	(1600)
10	FTE Teaching Staff (excluding TA)	(30.00)	(39.39)
11	FTE Research Staff (excluding RA)	(15.00)	(19.70)
12	FTE Staff Requiring Office Space	(60.00)	(78.78)
13	Instructional Lab Space Required		
	(Base Year) — 1200 × 4.25	5100	
	(19XX) — 1600 × 4.25		6800
14	Office Space Required		
	(Base Year) 60 × 135	8100	
	(19XX) 78.78 × 135		10635

Line No.		Base Year	Projected Year 19XX
15	FTE Teaching Staff 39.39 × 3 = 118.17		
16	FTE Research Staff 19.70 × 15 = 295.50		
17	Headcount Beg. Grad. 66 × 3 = 198.00		
18	Headcount Adv. Grad. 66 × 15 = 990.00		
19	Total Research Demand Units = 1601.67		
20	Research Space 1601.67 × 25 (RDF)	26775	40042
21	Subtotal Department Space	39975	57477
22	Archive and Research Equip. Storage One Per Cent	400	575
23	Department Total	40375	58052
24	Classroom Space Generated by Department 1965 (1000 × .833) 19XX − 1400 × .833	833	1166

The data enclosed in parentheses for the base year are known values. The data enclosed in parentheses for the projected year are enrollment projections which it is assumed will exist. From these data, the weekly student hours for classroom and laboratory, lines 8 and 9, may be calculated based upon previous trend data on the distribution of course work by courses to the various departments dependent upon the mix of students by level throughout the university. The staff, items 10, 11, and 12, may be projected using the institution's staff multiplier. In this example it would be:

$$\frac{\text{Projected year}}{\text{Base year}} = \frac{\frac{130}{18} + \frac{200}{12} + \frac{50}{9} + \frac{50}{4}}{\frac{120}{18} + \frac{160}{12} + \frac{40}{9} + \frac{30}{4}} = 1.313$$

The projected instructional laboratory space, line 13, is obtained by multiplying the weekly student hours, line 9, times the square feet per weekly student hour for chemistry.

The projected office space, line 14, is obtained by multiplying the FTE staff requiring office space, line 12, times 135. The research space is obtained by multiplying the research demand units, the sum of lines 15, 16, 17, and 18, times the departmental research demand factor. The remainder of the calculations are self-explanatory.

From these data, it is possible to determine the office space, laboratory space, and classroom space generated by the department. Other calculations of "building blocks" such as library space, inactive space, physical plant space, etc. are done on a total university enrollment basis rather than on a departmental basis.

Once the calculation of facilities is completed, the next task is to effectively summarize and tabulate the data for each administrative unit and academic department. Table 9 gives a proposed format with an example of data for a portion of a hypothetical Fine and Applied Arts College.

These data indicate that the existing facilities for the Fine and Applied Arts Administration and the Department of Art are adequate for the projected

Table 9. Example of a Format for Presenting the Space Requirements for a Portion of a Hypothetical Fine and Applied Arts College All Values in Net Assignable Square Feet

Department	Year	Instr. Lab.	Office	Research Lab	Archive and Storage	Total
FAA	1965 [a]		1,100		165	1,265
Administration	1965		980		98	1,078
	1967		1,000		100	1,100
	1969		1,040		104	1,144
	1971		1,060		106	1,166
	1973		1,100		110	1,210
	1975		1,140		114	1,254
	1977		1,180		118	1,298
	1979		1,200		120	1,320
Architecture	1965 [a]	31,104	8,430	4,979	347	44,860
	1965	32,415	8,427	5,036	459	46,337
	1967	33,555	8,873	5,343	478	48,249
	1969	35,399	9,441	5,685	505	51,030
	1971	37,728	9,991	5,961	537	54,217
	1973	38,782	10,324	6,176	553	55,835
	1975	40,770	10,970	6,660	584	58,984
	1977	41,971	11,338	7,124	603	60,856
	1979	44,428	11,932	7,533	639	64,532
Art	1965 [a]	69,322	7,930	21,080	950	99,282
	1965	61,833	6,618	12,306	808	81,565
	1967	62,633	6,844	16,291	853	86,621
	1969	64,026	7,126	16,967	881	89,000
	1971	66,549	7,399	17,950	919	92,817
	1973	67,638	7,706	18,753	941	95,038
	1975	69,240	7,947	20,022	972	98,181
	1977	69,660	8,141	21,458	993	100,252
	1979	75,456	8,588	22,494	1,065	107,603

[a] Existing.

enrollments through 1975. However, the Department of Architecture is short of facilities at the present time, and it will be necessary to provide additional facilities in the very near future. The calculation of facilities required by the "Numeric Method" gives a boundary condition of facilities required for the department based upon either an existing enrollment or projected enrollment. When a building is planned for a department it should be planned for an enrollment far enough in the future that after the building is constructed the department can expand as the enrollment increases. Thus the relationship of space available to a department will be on a stairstep basis, whereas the enrollment increases will follow more or less a curve function. Thus the department will usually have assigned to it more space than it generates or less space than it generates. It is the opinion of the authors that the educational program of a department will suffer materially if the space available is lower than 90 per cent of that generated. In this example, the Department of Architecture should have a building under construction or should be planning a building as soon as possible.

When the data by academic department and college, as shown in Table 9, are completed, it is highly desirable to prepare a summary of the data together with the general university facilities which are not assigned to a particular academic department. This summary will present the total physical facilities required by a university. The summary may be tabulated by major administrative units or by "building blocks." Table 10 gives an example of a format for tabulating the data of a hypothetical institution by major administrative units, and Table 11 gives an example of the same data tabulated by "building blocks." The data is presented in both ways because various offices on the campus have found this to be necessary.

The next step is to determine the additional facilities to be requested by comparing the projected physical facilities required with the existing facilities. Table 12 shows this comparison for a hypothetical institution. These data should provide the basis for the next capital budget request of a state-supported institution. The example assumes that preparations are being made for the 1967-69 capital budget request. As the data must be prepared and presented sometime in the year 1966, the base year data will be for the 1965 fall semester conditions. If planning money has not been made available for a capital project in the previous biennium, it will take from three to four years to prepare the drawings and construct a building after the money has been appropriated. Thus, assuming no planning money has been made available, facilities in the process of construction as a result of the capital budget allocation for 1965-67 will not be available to the institution until the fall of 1969. Those facilities requested for the 1967-69 biennium will not be available until the fall of 1971 and must serve the institution until the fall of 1973 as no new facilities will be provided until that time. The table is arranged to show the status as a result of the 1965-67 budget and additional space required as a result of changes in student mix and enrollment increase in 1973.

The values in Table 12 for columns 2 and 3, "1971 Required" and "1973 Required," are obtained from Table 10. The values for column 4, "1965 Existing," were obtained from the inventory of physical facilities obtained by procedures as discussed in Chapter 3. The values for column 5, "Open by Sept. 1969," are a summary of the projects which are under construction or have been approved for construction and are not yet included in the inventory. The procedure is not to include buildings on the inventory during the time of planning and construction, but to wait until the building is occupied and then include it on the inventory. The values in column 6, "Total Available Sept. 1969," summarizes the total space available as of the fall semester assuming the construction of all projects approved in the 1965-67 biennium will be completed. The values in column 7, "Additional Required 1971," gives the additional space required to 1971 and gives an idea of where the space problems will be arising during the coming biennium. The values in column 8, "Additional Required 1973," gives the amount of additional space required for 1973 and indicates the facilities that should be requested. From this type of summary the university can determine the net assignable square feet needed to accommodate the enrollments in educational programs projected. The summaries pinpoint the academic areas which need additional space and should serve as a basis for identifying the specific building projects request to be included in the next capital budget request.

With the data from Tables 9, 10, 11, and 12, the personnel responsible for developing a building program can formulate the specific building projects that should be put in the next biennial capital request. The deliberation on the projects to be included will involve an assessment of buildings that may have to be razed, either because they are on building sites or because they have been condemned for safety reasons, and the reassignment of space that may be vacated as a result of a department moving into a new building. After the specific projects have been determined, a summary sheet similar to Table 13 should be prepared to review the status of all space upon completion of the proposed building program. Columns 2 and 3 of Table 13 should be similar to columns 3 and 6 of Table 12. Column 4 gives that space which must be razed. Column 5 gives the result of the planned reassignment of space between the various colleges and administrative units. Note this is merely an interchange of space between units. Column 6 gives the space that is being requested for the next biennium. Column 7 summarizes the net effect of all of these space changes. It is the result of column 3 minus column 4 plus or minus column 5 plus column 6. Column 8 gives the surplus or shortages of space for each college or unit. It can be noted in the example of the data for the hypothetical institution that the space requested does not provide a complete numerical balance between the facilities generated and those available. The reason for this can again be explained by the stairstep effect of the provision of space by a building and the curve effect of the procedure for generating space.

Table 10. *Example of a Summary of the Physical Facilities Required for a Hypothetical Institution by Major Administrative Units for the Years 1965-79 All Values in Net Assignable Square Feet*

	1965	1967	1969	1971	1973	1975	1977	1979
Administration	250,054	263,193	274,113	285,433	296,834	306,885	320,490	337,071
Agriculture	365,546	374,511	385,685	399,048	413,440	430,335	443,206	467,521
Commerce	37,652	40,365	42,266	44,423	46,577	48,242	50,308	53,461
Education	82,603	87,234	91,789	96,927	102,381	108,085	113,816	121,792
Engineering	717,197	778,084	814,936	861,797	913,079	967,641	1,015,049	1,088,734
FAA	233,810	249,137	257,901	268,997	277,289	285,737	294,373	314,913
Graduate College	55,193	53,269	54,243	62,090	63,436	64,817	66,176	83,247
Journalism	28,165	29,712	30,872	32,149	33,332	34,185	35,088	37,204
Law	17,040	17,697	23,312	26,155	26,529	26,945	27,485	27,781
LAS	808,530	828,569	855,635	888,979	931,382	980,898	1,025,483	1,092,111
Physical Education	202,676	199,046	197,469	196,267	196,332	198,765	201,227	209,678
University Extension	20,050	20,688	21,328	21,981	22,711	23,287	24,014	24,976
Veterinary Medicine	125,073	130,036	141,572	162,644	182,354	195,374	199,180	203,001
Military Science	21,101	21,355	21,550	21,716	21,938	21,958	22,111	22,505
Misc. Depts.	18,578	20,528	21,292	22,287	23,340	24,499	26,502	28,220
Gen. Univ. (Armory Floor)	73,922	73,922	73,922	73,922	73,922	73,922	73,922	73,922
Subtotal	3,057,190	3,187,346	3,307,885	3,464,815	3,624,876	3,791,575	3,938,430	4,186,137
Classroom	282,040	289,970	300,166	310,695	318,135	324,565	335,036	356,305
Library	625,870	669,494	712,919	754,657	795,895	837,411	880,395	929,581
Commons	41,828	43,356	44,498	45,677	47,060	48,420	50,046	52,641
Inactive	58,995	61,744	64,373	67,529	70,681	73,922	76,950	81,761
Physical Plant	173,703	185,079	193,713	201,608	209,435	217,137	224,883	238,053
Subtotal	4,239,626	4,436,989	4,623,554	4,844,981	5,066,082	5,293,030	5,505,740	5,844,478
Student Services	237,287	245,743	254,331	262,284	270,311	278,132	287,298	301,612
Hospital	43,143	44,681	46,242	47,688	49,148	50,570	52,236	54,839
Lab School	39,875	39,875	39,875	39,875	39,875	39,875	39,875	39,875
Museum	41,786	41,786	41,786	41,786	41,786	41,786	41,786	41,786
Gym NFI	119,676	119,676	119,676	119,676	119,676	119,676	119,676	119,676
Aud. NFI	288,925	288,925	288,925	288,925	288,925	288,925	288,925	288,925
Athletic Association	108,890	108,890	108,890	108,890	108,890	108,890	108,890	108,890
Quasi University	161,296	161,296	161,296	161,296	161,296	161,296	161,296	161,296
Total	5,280,504	5,487,861	5,684,575	5,915,401	6,145,989	6,382,180	6,605,722	6,961,377

Table 11. Example of a Summary of the Physical Facilities Required for a Hypothetical Institution by "Building Blocks" for the Years 1965-79
All Values in Net Assignable Square Feet

	1965	1967	1969	1971	1973	1975	1977	1979
Classroom	282,040	289,970	300,166	310,695	318,135	324,565	335,036	356,305
Instructional Lab	718,535	733,223	750,985	780,435	803,403	826,009	840,376	887,401
Office	960,051	1,002,195	1,041,829	1,090,121	1,134,875	1,175,923	1,224,534	1,300,233
Library	625,870	669,494	712,919	754,657	795,895	837,411	880,395	929,581
Research	1,071,156	1,132,747	1,183,663	1,249,529	1,329,416	1,421,062	1,492,522	1,600,256
Commons	51,436	53,151	56,768	59,865	62,072	63,940	65,872	68,560
Archive Storage	223,918	235,464	245,216	256,620	268,248	279,139	291,250	308,406
Inactive	58,995	61,744	64,373	67,529	70,681	73,922	76,950	81,761
Buildings and Grounds	173,703	185,079	193,713	201,608	209,435	217,137	224,883	238,053
Gen. Univ. (Armory Floor)	73,922	73,922	73,922	73,922	73,922	73,922	73,922	73,922
Subtotal	4,239,626	4,436,989	4,623,554	4,844,981	5,066,082	5,293,030	5,505,740	5,844,478
Student Services	237,287	245,743	254,331	262,284	270,311	278,132	287,298	301,612
Hospital	43,143	44,681	46,242	47,688	49,148	50,570	52,236	54,839
Lab School	39,875	39,875	39,875	39,875	39,875	39,875	39,875	39,875
Museum	41,786	41,786	41,786	41,786	41,786	41,786	41,786	41,786
Gym NFI	119,676	119,676	119,676	119,676	119,676	119,676	119,676	119,676
Aud. NFI	288,925	288,925	288,925	288,925	288,925	288,925	288,925	288,925
Athletic Association	108,890	108,890	108,890	108,890	108,890	108,890	108,890	108,890
Quasi University	161,296	161,296	161,296	161,296	161,296	161,296	161,296	161,296
Total	5,280,504	5,487,861	5,684,575	5,915,401	6,145,989	6,382,180	6,605,722	6,961,377

Table 12. *Example of a Comparison of the Physical Facilities required by General Administration and Each Major Unit of a Hypothetical Institution in 1971 and 1973 with That Presently Existing and That Under Construction Which Will Be Completed by Fall 1969*
All Values in Net Assignable Square Feet

(1) Program or Function	(2) 1971 Required	(3) 1973 Required	(4) 1965 Existing	(5) Open by Sept. 1969	(6) Total Available Sept. 1969	(7) Add. Req'd 1971	(8) Add. Req'd 1973
Administration	285,433	296,834	232,802	25,739	258,541	26,892	38,293
Agriculture	399,048	413,440	400,081	–0–	400,081	(1,033)	13,359
Commerce	44,423	46,577	48,744	–0–	48,744	(4,321)	(2,167)
Education	96,927	102,381	85,483	–0–	85,483	11,444	16,898
Engineering	861,797	913,079	801,669	98,326	899,995	(38,198)	13,084
FAA	268,997	277,289	185,813	63,197	249,010	19,987	28,279
Graduate College	62,090	63,436	76,213	–0–	76,213	(14,123)	(12,777)
Journalism	32,149	33,332	29,971	–0–	29,971	2,178	3,361
Law	26,155	26,529	14,834	–0–	14,834	11,321	11,695
LAS	888,979	931,382	743,106	128,538	871,644	17,335	59,738
Physical Education	196,267	196,332	195,461	–0–	195,461	806	871
University Extension	21,981	22,711	18,479	909	19,388	2,593	3,323
Veterinary Medicine	162,644	182,354	60,643	120,562	181,205	(18,561)	1,149
Military Science	21,716	21,938	22,406	–0–	22,406	(690)	(468)
Misc. Depts.	22,287	23,340	21,995	–0–	21,995	292	1,345
Gen. Univ. (Armory Floor)	73,922	73,922	73,922	–0–	73,922	–0–	–0–
Subtotal A	3,464,815	3,624,876	3,011,622	437,271	3,448,893	15,922	175,983
Classrooms	310,695	318,135	305,718	20,651	326,369	(15,674)	(8,234)
Library	754,657	795,895	416,490	227,597	644,087	110,570	151,808
Commons	45,677	47,060	30,677	8,877	39,554	6,123	7,506
Inactive	67,529	70,681	48,250	3,734	51,984	15,545	18,697
Physical Plant	201,608	209,435	165,523	–0–	165,523	36,085	43,912
Subtotal B	4,844,981	5,066,082	3,978,280	698,130	4,676,410	168,571	389,672
Student Services	262,284	270,311	168,753	–0–	168,753	93,531	101,558
Hospital	47,688	49,148	36,906	–0–	36,906	10,782	12,242
Lab School	39,875	39,875	39,875	–0–	39,875	–0–	–0–
Museum	41,786	41,786	41,786	–0–	41,786	–0–	–0–
Gym NFI	119,676	119,676	44,250	75,426	119,676	–0–	–0–
Aud. NFI	288,925	288,925	193,712	95,213	288,925	–0–	–0–
Athletic Association	108,890	108,890	108,890	–0–	108,890	–0–	–0–
Quasi University	161,296	161,296	161,296	–0–	161,296	–0–	–0–
Total	5,915,401	6,145,989	4,773,748	868,769	5,642,517	272,884	503,472

Table 13. *Example of a Status of Space Upon Completion of a 1967-69 Building Program for a Hypothetical Institution All Values in Net Assignable Square Feet*

(1) Program or Function	(2) Space Req'd 1973	(3) Space Available 1969	(4) Space To Be Razed	(5) Space Gained (+) or Lost (−) by Reassignment	(6) Space Requested in 1967-69 Budget	(7) Net Amount of Space To Be Available 1973	(8) Surplus (+) Shortage (−) in 1973
Administration	296,834	258,541	−0−	−8,672	47,762	297,631	+797
Agriculture	413,440	400,081	10,113	−25,624	50,624	414,968	+1,528
Commerce	46,577	48,744	−0−	−0−	−0−	48,744	+2,167
Education	102,381	85,483	5,513	+21,617	−0−	101,587	−794
Engineering	913,079	899,995	20,716	−0−	31,710	910,989	−2,090
FAA	277,289	249,010	3,520	−0−	22,600	268,090	−9,199
Graduate College	63,436	76,213	−0−	−11,208	−0−	65,005	+1,569
Journalism	33,332	29,971	−0−	+4,312	−0−	34,283	+951
Law	26,529	14,834	−0−	−0−	14,821	29,655	+3,126
LAS	931,382	871,644	23,212	+37,484	44,610	930,526	−856
Physical Education	196,332	195,461	−0−	−0−	−0−	195,461	−871
University Extension	22,711	19,388	−0−	+3,212	−0−	22,600	−111
Veterinary Medicine	182,354	181,205	−0−	−0−	−0−	181,205	−1,149
Military Science	21,938	22,406	−0−	−0−	−0−	22,406	+468
Misc. Depts.	23,340	21,995	−0−	+1,461	−0−	23,456	+116
Gen. Univ. (Armory Floor)	73,922	73,922	−0−	−0−	−0−	73,922	−0−
Subtotal A	3,624,876	3,448,893	63,074	+22,582	212,127	3,620,528	−4,348
Classrooms	318,135	326,369	1,600	−21,617	14,612	317,764	−371
Library	795,895	644,087	−0−	−0−	122,612	766,699	−29,196
Commons	47,060	39,554	−0−	−0−	5,020	44,574	−2,486
Inactive (Remodel)	70,681	51,984	−0−	−965	−0−	51,019	−19,662
Physical Plant	209,435	165,523	−0−	−0−	46,716	212,239	+2,804
Subtotal B	5,066,082	4,676,410	64,674	−0−	401,087	5,012,823	−53,259
Student Services	270,311	168,753	−0−	−0−	112,762	281,515	+11,204
Hospital	49,148	36,906	−0−	−0−	−0−	36,906	−12,242
Lab School	39,875	39,875	−0−	−0−	−0−	39,875	−0−
Museum	41,786	41,786	−0−	−0−	−0−	41,786	−0−
Gym NFI	119,676	119,676	−0−	−0−	−0−	119,676	−0−
Aud. NFI	288,925	288,925	−0−	−0−	−0−	288,925	−0−
Athletic Association	108,890	108,890	−0−	−0−	−0−	108,890	−0−
Quasi University	161,296	161,296	−0−	−0−	−0−	161,296	−0−
Total	6,145,989	5,642,517	64,674	−0−	513,849	6,091,692	−54,297

PLANNING OF SPECIFIC CAPITAL OUTLAY PROJECTS

The foregoing chapters have provided a methodology for the analysis of existing facilities and for the projection of physical facilities requirements. In addition, suggestions have been made regarding the presentation of data for effective use. This chapter discusses some of the specific steps involved in planning those projects that have been selected to satisfy the space deficiencies indicated by the foregoing methodologies.

The space computation by the "Numeric Method" resulted in establishing the total net assignable square feet required by each academic department. This forms a "boundary condition" for space to be planned into a building for a department for a given enrollment in a specific year. However, before establishing the total size of a capital project, general university space such as classrooms, library, and commons facilities must be considered together with existing space assigned to a department at the time the project is completed.

The total classroom and libary space included in a project should be analyzed on a total campus basis — not a departmental basis. The number and size of classrooms should be viewed in terms of meeting the total campus need. This should also be the case for library space, even though branch libraries are planned on a departmental basis. The total of the departmental libraries, in conjunction with the main library, should not exceed that which is needed for the campus enrollment.

Another consideration in determining the size of a capital project is that of future expansion for departmental and general university facilities. It should be mentioned that the lapse time from the conception of a building to its occupancy is from four to six years. The six-year time period is becoming more and more common if requests are to be made for federal grants. With a six-year planning and construction period, the building should be planned to include facilities for an additional four years after occupancy. Thus if a building is being considered for inclusion in the 1967-69 budget, it should be planned to accommodate the departments to be in the building until 1977.

Because planning a new building affects a large number of people, it is recommended that a memorandum be sent to the university administrator who is responsible for approving planning on capital projects requesting permission to prepare a planning document called a program statement. This memorandum should contain the following:

1. Names of the departments to be included in the building.
2. The net assignable square feet generated by the "Numeric Method" for each "building block."
3. The projected enrollment by level of student for the projected year.
4. The resulting staff projections based on the above enrollment breakdown.
5. A summary of the existing space which will be vacated at the time of occupancy.
6. A rough cost estimate of the project.
7. Signatures of those directly involved in the initial planning of the building. They are as follows:
    a. Project coordinator
    b. Head of department
    c. Dean of college
    d. Director of planning

This memorandum is the agreement between the administration, the college, and the academic department as to the amount of space that is required and the facilities that will be released for assignment to other academic departments within the university if this project is constructed. An example of a memorandum requesting permission to prepare a program statement is shown in Appendix C.

If approval is given, this memorandum should be distributed to all administrative offices involved in planning. At this time the planning officer will commence working with the users of the proposed building to develop a program statement which will form the basis from which an architect can start the schematic drawings. The program statement should contain the following data:

1. A general statement with regard to (1) why the project is proposed; (2) what the project is intended to accomplish; and (3) a brief summary of the types of facilities to be included.
2. A statement of general considerations that affect various aspects of the site, design, bid documents, timetable, and budget.
3. A summary of total space needs, listing area code, description of room, and square feet.
4. A chart indicating the spatial and functional relationship of related areas.

5. A description of the specific requirements of special or fixed equipment or utilities and movable equipment or furniture.

An example of a program statement for a foreign languages building at the University of Illinois is given in Appendix D. A further detailed discussion does not appear to be warranted because each building project is presented in a slightly different manner and there are many different ways of presenting the same material.

When a preliminary draft of the program statement is completed by the planning officer and the users of the proposed building, it should be sent to (1) the campus architect's office if there is one, or some outside architectural firm for preparation of building cost estimates and the construction timetable; (2) the Physical Plant Department for computation of off-site costs such as utilities extension and landscaping costs; (3) all the users of the proposed facility for assurance of complete agreement on the contents. When the above information is compiled and agreed upon, the final draft of the program statement should be prepared and distributed to:

1. President
2. Vice-President(s)
3. Dean of college
4. Academic departments included in project
5. Campus architect's office
6. Project architectural firm
7. Physical Plant Department

As indicated, the program statement provides a basis for preparing preliminary drawings by the project architect. It should be regarded as a goal for arriving at an acceptable set of preliminary drawings as it sets forth the general facilities requested with the specific details to be worked out in conferences with the university staff.

Once the program statement is given to the project architect, the planning officer must be kept informed of the status of the project at the various stages of planning. For the purpose of compiling reports and keeping the administrative officials informed, it is suggested that a review of the space programmed by "building blocks" and room designation be compared with the drawings at the following stages of planning:

1. Prior to the submission of the schematic drawings for any grant application.
2. Prior to the preparation of final preliminary drawings.
3. After working drawings are completed.
4. At the time of occupancy. (This will be an addition to the physical facilities inventory.)

Appendix E presents a form to facilitate the status reviews. The steps involved in coordinating the planning activity between the university staff and the project architect are usually determined by previous understandings between the two parties and will vary from project to project.

In the early stages in planning, close surveillance must be given to the relationship of net assignable square feet to gross square feet. If a low ratio of net assignable square feet to gross square feet is not discovered until the final phase of the working drawings, only two alternatives are available — either continue the drawings or spend time and expense on redesign.

Basically, there are two ways of referring to the relationship of net assignable square feet to gross square feet. They are *building efficiency* and *add factor*. Both are interrelated, and in determining either one of the relationships, the other will automatically result. Building efficiency is the ratio of net assignable area to gross area expressed as a percentage. The add factor is the amount of nonassignable space (circulation, construction, mechanical, restrooms, custodial) which must be included in a building in addition to the net assignable area, and it is expressed as a percentage of the net assignable square feet.

Thus, if it is stated that the add factor is 60 per cent, the building efficiency is 62.5 per cent; and if the add factor is 40 per cent, the building efficiency is 71.4 per cent. An illustration of these relationships is shown for a building having 50,000 net assignable square feet with an add factor of 40 per cent.

Net assignable square feet	50,000
Add factor, 40 per cent (40 per cent of 50,000 for circulation, mechanical, walls, etc.)	20,000
Gross square feet	70,000
Building efficiency	$\frac{50,000}{70,000} = 71.4$ per cent

The authors recommend use of the term building efficiency. However, as both terms are used in building construction and there have been instances of confusion when persons thought the terms were interchangeable, it is believed that a discussion of the two terms is necessary. The following indicates the relationship between building efficiency and add factor.

Add Factor to Net Assignable Square Feet in Per Cent of Net Assignable Square Feet	Building Efficiency in Per Cent of Gross Square Feet	Add Factor to Net Assignable Square Feet in Per Cent of Net Assignable Square Feet	Building Efficiency in Per Cent of Gross Square Feet
5	95.2	55	64.5
10	90.9	60	62.5
15	86.9	65	60.6
20	83.3	70	58.8
25	80.0	75	57.1
30	76.9	80	55.5
35	74.0	85	54.0
40	71.4	90	52.6
45	68.9	95	51.2
50	66.7	100	50.0

Very little has been written about building efficiency and the factors which affect building efficiency. Reports submitted to the U.S. Office of Education over the last ten years indicate that there has been a gradual trend toward a decreasing building efficiency. As a result of these trends some institutions and state agencies have conducted studies on buildings completed or being designed. These studies have indicated that the best way to evaluate building efficiency is by analyzing the portions of the building area committed to nonassignable areas. The initial studies have shown that the mechanical areas, other than restrooms, and the circulation and construction areas comprise the greatest amount of nonassignable area. However, because of the small number of samples taken in the studies, the percentage variations were quite large. It is the opinion of the authors that an interrelationship exists between the circulation and construction areas, and their combined value will depend upon the average size of room that is being planned within the building, i.e., as the average size of the room decreases the combined value of construction and circulation areas will increase. As a result of the initial studies made by the authors, which are not conclusive, the following guidelines on percentages of nonassignable space are provided for the analysis of building efficiencies.

Custodial. Janitor rooms will be approximately 0.4 per cent of the total gross square feet in the average academic building.

Mechanical. Mechanical areas will range from 3 per cent to 14 per cent of the total gross square feet depending upon whether or not the building is air conditioned or whether it contains environmental control equipment. This type of space will average approximately eight per cent of the building's gross square feet for air conditioned buildings. For those buildings having considerable fume hoods which require a separate exhaust system, a four to six per cent increase in mechanical space usually results.

Restrooms. Restroom space in the typical academic building will average 1.4 per cent of the total gross square feet. Buildings such as union buildings and those where spectator seating is included are not to be considered typical academic buildings.

Circulation. Corridors, stairs, and elevator shafts will average approximately 16 per cent of the total gross square feet in a building. This type of space will fluctuate, depending on the function of the building. At the lower end of the range will be library buildings and at the upper end of the range will be scheduled instructional facilities, such as classrooms and laboratories. It is recommended that further analysis be undertaken when the circulation space exceeds 16 per cent of the total gross square feet in the building.

Construction. Construction space will be approximately 14 per cent of the total gross square feet of an average academic building. Buildings with few interior partitions, such as library and physical education buildings with a small number of rooms, will appear at the top of the range.

APPENDIX A

FACULTY CODE AND ABBREVIATIONS USED FOR DESCRIPTION OF SPACE

Code	Abbreviation	Facility
010	Class Rm	Classroom
030	Lecture	Lecture Room or Assembly Hall
050	Seminar	Seminar Room
070	Office	Office
130	Lab	Laboratory
140	Court Rm	Court Room
150	Conf Rm	Conference Room
170	Counsel	Counseling Room
180	Clinic	Clinic
190	Field B	Field Buildings
210	Practice	Practice Rooms
230	Off Stud	Office Studio
240	Interv	Interview Room
250	Reading	Library Reading Room
260	Carrels	Library Carrels
270	Stacks	Library Stacks
280	Study	Library Study Room
290	Exhibit	Exhibition Room or Museum
300	Arena	Arena
310	Athletic	Athletic Activity Room
320	Activity	Student Activity Room
330	Gym	Gymnasium
370	Audit	Auditorium
390	Studio	Broadcasting Studio and Photo
400	Art Studio	Art Studio
410	Pool	Swimming Pool
420	Post Off	Post Office
430	Greenhse	Greenhouse
450	Seating	Spectator Seating
470	Recreatn	Recreation Room (Bowling, Ball, Billiard)
480	Drill	Drill Area
500	Shop	Shop
510	Study Sl	Study and Sleeping
520	Dorm Slp	Dormitory Type Sleeping
530	Bedroom	Patient's Bedroom or Ward and Allerton House Bedrooms

FACULTY CODE AND ABBREVIATIONS USED FOR DESCRIPTION OF SPACE

Code	Abbreviation	Facility
540	Apt	Apartment
550	Rest Rm	Rest Room
560	Toilet	Toilet
580	Dining	Dining Room
600	Cafeter	Cafeteria
620	Serving	Serving Line
640	Kitchen	Kitchen
660	Lounge	Lounge
670	Stall	Stalls
680	Canteen	Snack Bar or Canteen
690	Remodel	Remodeling or Unassigned
710	Animal	Animal Rentention or Experiment Room
711	Apparat	Lab Apparatus Room
712	Balance	Balance Room
713	Prepar	Preparation Room
714	Cent & O	Centrifuge and Oven Room
715	Cleaning	Lab Equipment Cleaning Room
718	Compute	Computation Room
719	Con Cur	Concrete Curing Room
720	Con Hum	Constant Humidity Room
721	Con Temp	Constant Temperature Room
722	Control	Control Panel or Room
723	Cr & Gr	Crushing, Grinding, and Polishing Room
724	Culture	Culture Room
725	Distill	Distillation Room
726	Drying	Drying or Dessicator Room
727	Engine	Engine Room
729	Feces Co	Feces Collecting Room
731	Glass Wk	Glass Working and Glass Blowing Room
732	Heat Tr	Heat Treatment Room
734	Hydrogen	Hydrogenation Room
735	Incubat	Incubator Room
736	Inspect	Inspection Room
737	Instrum	Instrument Room
738	Isolat	Isolation Room or Ward
739	Kjeldahl	Kjeldahl Room
740	Incine	Incinerator Room
742	Metabol	Metabolism Room
744	Obsvtn	Observation Room
745	Operat	Operating Room
746	Photo El	Photo Elastic Lab and Photo Lab
748	Refrig	Refrigeration or Cold Storage Room
751	Sound Pr	Sound Lock or Sound Proof Room
752	Steril	Sterilization or Autoclave Room
753	Transmis	Transmission Room
754	X-Ray	X-Ray Room
755	Aquaria	Aquarium
771	Compos	Composing Room — Printing Shop
772	Mill Rm	Mill Room — Wood or Metal Shop
781	Closet	Closets and Coat Rooms
782	Dark Rm	Dark Room
783	Dressing	Dressing Room
784	Locker	Storage Lockers
785	Receive	Material Receiving

FACULTY CODE AND ABBREVIATIONS USED FOR DESCRIPTION OF SPACE

Code	Abbreviation	Facility
786	Receptn	Reception
787	Storage	Storage Room
788	Vault	Storage Vault
789	Work Rm	Work Room or Projection Room
791	Book St	Book Storage — University Book Store
794	Pantry	Pantries
796	Tank Rm	Water and Liquid Storage Tanks
797	Obsvtn	Observation Room ⎫ ⎧ Other than
798	Sound Pr	Sound Proof Room ⎭ ⎩ Lab Auxiliary
799	Control	Control Room
811	Project	Projection Booth
812	Stage	Stage
840	File Rm	File Room
841	Wash Rm	Wash Room
842	Cashier	Cashier Booth
871	Dishwash	Dishwashing Room
872	Laundry	Laundry Room
891	First Ad	First Aid Room
892	Drying	Drying Room
894	Shower	Shower Room
895	Skate Sh	Skate Sharpening Room
896	Towel	Towel and Equipment Room
897	Training	Training Room
898	Ticket	Ticket Room or Booths
899	Coach	Coach's Room (not Office)
900	Lamp Rm	Light Bulb Storage
910	Battery	Battery Charging and Storage
911	Compress	Compressor Room
912	Elect Eq	Electrical Equipment Room
913	Fan Rm	Fan Room
914	Garage	Garage
915	Hv Equip	Heavy Equipment Room
916	Janitor	Janitor's Room
917	Mech Eq	Mechanical Equipment Room
918	Pipe Rm	Pipe Tunnel, Shaft, or Room
919	Power Rm	Power Room
920	Pump Rm	Pump Room
921	Switchbd	Switchboard Room
922	Telephon	Telephone Repair and Equipment Room
923	Teletype	Teletype Room
924	Transfor	Transformer Room
925	Well Rm	Well Room
930	HSG Aux	Housing Auxiliary
997	Corridor	Corridor
998	Stairwel	Stairwell
999	Elevator	Elevator

APPENDIX B

I - 1 - INVENTORY OF SPACE BY BUILDING   PAGE   6

BLDG. NO.	BLDG. NAME	ROOM NO.	AREA	CAPACITY	DEPT. CODE	DEPT. NAME	FAC. CODE	FAC. DESCR.	SCHED. NO.	COS NO.
001	DAVENP	0337A *	40		15150	AGRON	10070	OFFICE	0403	1111
001	DAVENP	0337B	270	3	15150	AGRON	30130	LAB	1200	1115
001	DAVENP	0338 *	296	0	15150	AGRON	30130	LAB	1200	1130
001	DAVENP	0338 *	40		15150	AGRON	10070	OFFICE	0403	1131
001	DAVENP	0338B	98	0	15150	AGRON	30130	LAB	1200	1135
001	DAVENP	0381	282		32660	PSYCH	10150	CONF RM	0402	1400
001	DAVENP	0382	113		32660	PSYCH	10070	OFFICE	0401	1405
001	DAVENP	0382A	160		32660	PSYCH	10070	OFFICE	0401	1410
001	DAVENP	0382B	68		32660	PSYCH	30130	LAB	1200	1415
001	DAVENP	0383	114		32660	PSYCH	10070	OFFICE	0401	1420
001	DAVENP	0385	120		32660	PSYCH	10070	OFFICE	0401	1425
001	DAVENP	0386A	81		32660	PSYCH	30130	LAB	1200	1430
001	DAVENP	0386B	126		32660	PSYCH	30130	LAB	1200	1435
001	DAVENP	0386C	95		32660	PSYCH	30130	LAB	1200	1440
001	DAVENP	0387	120		32660	PSYCH	10070	OFFICE	0401	1445
001	DAVENP	0389	114		32660	PSYCH	10070	OFFICE	0401	1450
001	DAVENP	0390A	78		32660	PSYCH	30130	LAB	1200	1455
001	DAVENP	0390	169		32660	PSYCH	30130	LAB	1200	1460
001	DAVENP	0390B	95		32660	PSYCH	30130	LAB	1200	1465
001	DAVENP	0390C	115		32660	PSYCH	10070	OFFICE	0401	1470
001	DAVENP	0390D	91		32660	PSYCH	30130	LAB	1200	1475
001	DAVENP	0391	138		32660	PSYCH	10070	OFFICE	0401	1480
001	DAVENP	0393	301		32660	PSYCH	30130	LAB	1200	1485
001	DAVENP	0396	270		32660	PSYCH	10070	OFFICE	0401	1490
001	DAVENP	0396A	219		32660	PSYCH	10789	WORK RM	0402	1495
001	DAVENP	0396B	167		32660	PSYCH	10070	OFFICE	0401	1500
001	DAVENP	0396C	121		32660	PSYCH	10070	OFFICE	0401	1505

277 NUMBER OF ROOMS

68753 BUILDING TOTAL

I 2 - INVENTORY OF SPACE BY DEPARTMENT   PAGE 106

BLDG. NO.	BLDG. NAME	ROOM NO.	AREA	CAPACITY	DEPT. CODE	DEPT. NAME	FAC. CODE	FAC. DESCR.	SCHED. NO.	COS NO.
002	FOR SL	0203A *	100		15550	FOR	10070	OFFICE	0401	0129
002	FOR SL	0204	386		15550	FOR	10070	OFFICE	0401	0134
002	FOR SL	0205	1229		15550	FOR	30130	LAB	0200	0139
002	FOR SL	0206	624		15550	FOR	10070	OFFICE	0401	0146
			7502 BUILDING TOTAL							
069	MUM H	0211	156	0	15550	FOR	10070	OFFICE	0401	0315
069	MUM H	0211A	144	0	15550	FOR	10070	OFFICE	0401	0320
069	MUM H	0211B	168	0	15550	FOR	10070	OFFICE	0401	0325
069	MUM H	0211C	156	0	15550	FOR	10070	OFFICE	0401	0330
069	MUM H	0215	202	2	15550	FOR	10070	OFFICE	0401	0350
069	MUM H	0216	195	2	15550	FOR	10070	OFFICE	0401	0355
069	MUM H	0217	195	2	15550	FOR	10070	OFFICE	0401	0360
069	MUM H	0219	195	2	15550	FOR	10070	OFFICE	0401	0375
069	MUM H	0220	195	1	15550	FOR	10070	OFFICE	0401	0380
069	MUM H	0222	180	2	15550	FOR	10070	OFFICE	0401	0390
			1786 BUILDING TOTAL							
158	BEVIER	0392	430		15550	FOR	30130	LAB	1200	0775
158	BEVIER	0396	464		15550	FOR	30130	LAB	1200	0785
158	BEVIER	0399	152		15550	FOR	10070	OFFICE	0401	0790
158	BEVIER	0399A	290		15550	FOR	10070	OFFICE	0401	0795
			1336 BUILDING TOTAL							
197	TURNER	W223 ¤	528		15550	FOR	30130	LAB	0200	0712
			528 BUILDING TOTAL							
			11152 DEPARTMENT TOTAL							

I 11 - CLASSROOMS   PAGE 18

DEPT. CODE	BLDG. CODE	COS CODE	BLDG. ABBREV.	ROOM NO.	AREA	FACILITY CODE	FACILITY DESCR.	SCHEDULE NUMBER
91100	069	0690	MUM H	405A	63	20787	STORAGE	0102
91100	069	0805	MUM H	442	493	20010	CLASSRM	0100
					5279	CLASSROOMS SCHEDULED		0100
					63	SERVICE TO CLASSROOMS		0102
					5342	BUILDING TOTAL		
91100	073	0130	D M B	203	400	20010	CLASSRM	0100
					400	CLASSROOMS SCHEDULED		0100
						SERVICE TO CLASSROOMS		0102
					400	BUILDING TOTAL		
91100	112	0100	M E B	56	500	20010	CLASSRM	0100
91100	112	0105	M E B	60	500	20010	CLASSRM	0100
91100	112	0110	M E B	64	500	20010	CLASSRM	0100
91100	112	0165	M E B	110	676	20010	CLASSRM	0100
91100	112	0250	M E B	136	520	20010	CLASSRM	0100
91100	112	0265	M E B	143A	500	20010	CLASSRM	0100
91100	112	0270	M E B	143B	500	20010	CLASSRM	0100
91100	112	0305	M E B	153A	500	20010	CLASSRM	0100
91100	112	0310	M E B	153B	500	20010	CLASSRM	0100
91100	112	0320	M E B	156	500	20010	CLASSRM	0100
91100	112	0325	M E B	160	580	20010	CLASSRM	0100
91100	112	0380	M E B	218	1180	20030	LECTURE	0100
91100	112	0450	M E B	236	520	20010	CLASSRM	0100
91100	112	0455	M E B	238	500	20010	CLASSRM	0100
91100	112	0460	M E B	242	500	20010	CLASSRM	0100
91100	112	0470	M E B	244	500	20010	CLASSRM	0100
91100	112	0475	M E B	248	440	20010	CLASSRM	0100
91100	112	0495	M E B	252	580	20010	CLASSRM	0100
91100	112	0500	M E B	253	1015	20030	LECTURE	0100
91100	112	0505	M E B	256	500	20010	CLASSRM	0100
91100	112	0510	M E B	260	580	20010	CLASSRM	0100
91100	112	0550	M E B	336	570	20010	CLASSRM	0100
91100	112	0570	M E B	344	532	20010	CLASSRM	0100
					13193	CLASSROOMS SCHEDULED		0100
						SERVICE TO CLASSROOMS		0102
					13193	BUILDING TOTAL		
91100	116	1028	E CHEM	101	608	20010	CLASSRM	0100
91100	116	1111	E CHEM	115	861	20010	CLASSRM	0100
91100	116	1113	E CHEM	116	2011	20030	LECTURE	0100
91100	116	2005	E CHEM	193	700	20010	CLASSRM	0100
91100	116	2027	E CHEM	199	589	20010	CLASSRM	0100
					4769	CLASSROOMS SCHEDULED		0100
						SERVICE TO CLASSROOMS		0102
					4769	BUILDING TOTAL		

I 12 - INSTRUCTIONAL LABORATORIES   PAGE   37

DEPT. CODE	BLDG. CODE	COS CODE	BLDG. ABBREV.	ROOM NO.	AREA	FACILITY CODE	FACILITY DESCR.	SCHEDULE NUMBER
24109	006	0598	ARMORY	247	1036	30130	LAB	0200
24109	006	1048	ARMORY	370	864	30130	LAB	0200
24109	006	1053	ARMORY	372	864	30130	LAB	0200
24109	006	1068	ARMORY	384	864	30130	LAB	0200
24109	006	1073	ARMORY	386	864	30130	LAB	0200
					4492	SCHEDULED LABORATORIES		0200
					973	AUXILIARY SPACE TO INSTRUCTION		1802
						HOSPITAL ROOMS TO INSTRUCTION		1803
						GREENHOUSE SPACE TO INSTRUCTION		1804
						ANIMAL ROOMS TO INSTRUCTION		1806
						ANIMAL STALLS TO INSTRUCTION		1808
					5465	BUILDING TOTAL		
24109	054	0075	D K H	24	1017	30130	LAB	0200
					1017	SCHEDULED LABORATORIES		0200
						AUXILIARY SPACE TO INSTRUCTION		1802
						HOSPITAL ROOMS TO INSTRUCTION		1803
						GREENHOUSE SPACE TO INSTRUCTION		1804
						ANIMAL ROOMS TO INSTRUCTION		1806
						ANIMAL STALLS TO INSTRUCTION		1808
					1017	BUILDING TOTAL		
24109	059	0005	SURV B	3	690	30130	LAB	0200
24109	059	0025	SURV B	103	869	30130	LAB	0200
24109	059	0040	SURV B	104	1000	30130	LAB	0200
24109	059	0065	SURV B	201	1176	30130	LAB	0200
24109	059	0070	SURV B	202	1064	30130	LAB	0200
					4799	SCHEDULED LABORATORIES		0200
					1262	AUXILIARY SPACE TO INSTRUCTION		1802
						HOSPITAL ROOMS TO INSTRUCTION		1803
						GREENHOUSE SPACE TO INSTRUCTION		1804
						ANIMAL ROOMS TO INSTRUCTION		1806
						ANIMAL STALLS TO INSTRUCTION		1808
					6061	BUILDING TOTAL		
24109	117	0065	N E L	152	440	30130	LAB	0200
					440	SCHEDULED LABORATORIES		0200
					850	AUXILIARY SPACE TO INSTRUCTION		1802
						HOSPITAL ROOMS TO INSTRUCTION		1803
						GREENHOUSE SPACE TO INSTRUCTION		1804
						ANIMAL ROOMS TO INSTRUCTION		1806
						ANIMAL STALLS TO INSTRUCTION		1808
					1290	BUILDING TOTAL		
24109	219	0005	F A B	9	1596	30130	LAB	0200

I-13 - INSTRUCTIONAL GYM, POOL, DRILL HALL   PAGE   8

DEPT. CODE	BLDG. CODE	COS CODE	BLDG. ABBREV.	ROOM NO.	AREA	FACILITY CODE	FACILITY DESCR.	SCHEDULE NUMBER
36209	044	0015	ENGL B	4A	112	30784	LOCKER	0302
36209	044	0020	ENGL B	4B	969	30784	LOCKER	0302
36209	044	0030	ENGL B	6A	126	30787	STORAGE	0302
36209	044	0035	ENGL B	6B	418	30782	DARK RM	0302
36209	044	0040	ENGL B	6C	220	30896	TOWEL	0302
36209	044	0050	ENGL B	8	2640	30784	LOCKER	0302
36209	044	0055	ENGL B	8A	160	30560	TOILET	0302
36209	044	0060	ENGL B	8B	1568	30784	LOCKER	0302
36209	044	0075	ENGL B	12	172	30896	TOWEL	0302
36209	044	0085	ENGL B	16	597	30894	SHOWER	0302
36209	044	0090	ENGL B	16C	88	30892	DRYING	0302
36209	044	0110	ENGL B	21	180	30783	DRESSING	0302
36209	044	0115	ENGL B	26	7680	30330	GYM	0300
36209	044	0310	ENGL B	116A	2958	30410	POOL	0300
36209	044	0325	ENGL B	118A	190	30784	LOCKER	0302
36209	044	0330	ENGL B	118B	105	30894	SHOWER	0302
36209	044	0520	ENGL B	218	4450	30330	GYM	0300
					15088		GYMS, POOLS AND DRILL HALLS	0300
					7545		SERVICE SPACE TO GYMS, ETC.	0302
					22633		BUILDING TOTAL	
36209	064	0003	WO GYM	10	1280	30390	STUDIO	0300
36209	064	0004	WO GYM	10C	64	30789	WORK RM	0302
36209	064	0005	WO GYM	11	3131	30330	GYM	0300
36209	064	0010	WO GYM	100	449	30789	WORK RM	0302
36209	064	0015	WO GYM	111	378	30787	STORAGE	0302
36209	064	0030	WO GYM	115B	77	30783	DRESSING	0302
36209	064	0060	WO GYM	118A	56	30783	DRESSING	0302
36209	064	0065	WO GYM	119	2250	30783	DRESSING	0302
36209	064	0070	WO GYM	119A	969	30894	SHOWER	0302
36209	064	0075	WO GYM	120	42	30787	STORAGE	0302
36209	064	0080	WO GYM	121	105	30787	STORAGE	0302
36209	064	0085	WO GYM	122	325	30784	LOCKER	0302
36209	064	0090	WO GYM	123	325	30784	LOCKER	0302
36209	064	0095	WO GYM	125	2655	30783	DRESSING	0302
36209	064	0100	WO GYM	125A	720	30894	SHOWER	0302
36209	064	0130	WO GYM	207A	195	30550	REST RM	0302
36209	064	0135	WO GYM	207B	260	30150	CONF RM	0302
36209	064	0170	WO GYM	213	96	30787	STORAGE	0302
36209	064	0175	WO GYM	214	96	30787	STORAGE	0302
36209	064	0180	WO GYM	215	1558	30330	GYM	0300
36209	064	0185	WO GYM	310	6222	30330	GYM	0300
36209	064	0190	WO GYM	310B	147	30787	STORAGE	0302
36209	064	0195	WO GYM	311	5063	30330	GYM	0300
36209	064	0200	WO GYM	311B	130	30787	STORAGE	0302
36209	064	0205	WO GYM	409	24	30787	STORAGE	0302
36209	064	0220	WO GYM	412	24	30787	STORAGE	0302
					17254		GYMS, POOLS AND DRILL HALLS	0300
					9387		SERVICE SPACE TO GYMS, ETC.	0302
					26641		BUILDING TOTAL	

APPENDIX B   **105**

I 14 - OFFICE SPACE   PAGE 246

DEPT. CODE	BLDG. CODE	COS CODE	BLDG. ABBREV.	ROOM NO.	AREA	FACILITY CODE	FACILITY DESCR.	SCHEDULE NUMBER
36250	006	0353	ARMORY	215	221	10070	OFFICE	0401
36250	006	0358	ARMORY	219A	98	10070	OFFICE	0401
36250	006	0363	ARMORY	220	175	10070	OFFICE	0401
36250	006	0368	ARMORY	220A	80	10070	OFFICE	0401
					574	OFFICE WITH OCCUPANTS		0401
						WORK, CONFERENCE, FILE SPACE		0402
						OFFICE SPACE IN LABS		0403
						STORAGE, CLOSETS, VAULTS		0404
					574	BUILDING TOTAL		
36250	058	0225	HUFF G	104	400	10070	OFFICE	0401
36250	058	0230	HUFF G	104A	30	10788	VAULT	0404
36250	058	0235	HUFF G	104B	75	10070	OFFICE	0401
36250	058	0240	HUFF G	104C	77	10070	OFFICE	0401
36250	058	0245	HUFF G	104D	143	10070	OFFICE	0401
36250	058	0250	HUFF G	104E	220	10070	OFFICE	0404
36250	058	0251	HUFF G	104F	200	10070	OFFICE	0401
36250	058	0380	HUFF G	203	145	10070	OFFICE	0401
36250	058	0385	HUFF G	203A	108	10070	OFFICE	0401
					1148	OFFICE WITH OCCUPANTS		0401
						WORK, CONFERENCE, FILE SPACE		0402
						OFFICE SPACE IN LABS		0403
					250	STORAGE, CLOSETS, VAULTS		0404
					1398	BUILDING TOTAL		
36250	075	0030	C R C	7 ¤	32	10150	CONF RM	0402
36250	075	0090	C R C	13 ¤	13	10150	CONF RM	0402
36250	075	0120	C R C	19 ¤	33	10787	STORAGE	0404
36250	075	0185	C R C	20B ¤	4	10787	STORAGE	0404
36250	075	0215	C R C	20C ¤	8	10787	STORAGE	0404
36250	075	0340	C R C	29 ¤	13	10070	OFFICE	0401
36250	075	0470	C R C	56	136	10787	STORAGE	0404
36250	075	0600	C R C	93	147	10070	OFFICE	0401
36250	075	0605	C R C	95	154	10070	OFFICE	0401
36250	075	0620	C R C	97	168	10070	OFFICE	0401
					482	OFFICE WITH OCCUPANTS		0401
					45	WORK, CONFERENCE, FILE SPACE		0402
						OFFICE SPACE IN LABS		0403
					181	STORAGE, CLOSETS, VAULTS		0404
					708	BUILDING TOTAL		
36250	205	0144	1203WO	301	182	10070	OFFICE	0401
36250	205	0151	1203WO	301A	18	10781	CLOSET	0404
36250	205	0154	1203WO	304	143	10070	OFFICE	0401
36250	205	0159	1203WO	304A	24	10787	STORAGE	0404
36250	205	0164	1203WO	305	154	10070	OFFICE	0401
36250	205	0171	1203WO	305A	20	10787	STORAGE	0404

I 15 - LIBRARY SPACE PAGE 6

DEPT. CODE	BLDG. CODE	COS CODE	BLDG. ABBREV.	ROOM NO.		AREA	FACILITY CODE	FACILITY DESCR.	SCHEDULE NUMBER
80500	012	0645	NOYES	163	*	285	40250	READING	0503
80500	012	0646	NOYES	163	*	547	40270	STACKS	0502
80500	012	0920	NOYES	257	*	912	40250	READING	0503
80500	012	0921	NOYES	257	*	150	10070	OFFICE	0509
80500	012	0922	NOYES	257	*	1062	40270	STACKS	0502
80500	012	0925	NOYES	257A	*	204	40250	READING	0503
80500	012	0926	NOYES	257A	*	366	40270	STACKS	0502
80500	012	0945	NOYES	260A	*	600	40270	STACKS	0502
80500	012	0946	NOYES	260A	*	600	40250	READING	0503
						2575		STACK AREA	0502
						2001		READING AND STUDY	0503
								CARRELS	0504
								SERVICE AREA	0506
						150		OFFICE SPACE	0509
						4726		BUILDING TOTAL	
80500	015	0130	ENG H	117		240	10789	WORK RM	0509
80500	015	0135	ENG H	118		224	10070	OFFICE	0509
80500	015	0140	ENG H	118A		173	10789	WORK RM	0506
80500	015	0145	ENG H	119	*	4070	40270	STACKS	0502
80500	015	0146	ENG H	119	*	165	10070	OFFICE	0509
80500	015	0150	ENG H	119B		96	10787	STORAGE	0509
80500	015	0155	ENG H	119C		84	10070	OFFICE	0509
80500	015	0269	ENG H	215		384	10070	OFFICE	0509
80500	015	0270	ENG H	215A		100	10070	OFFICE	0509
80500	015	0275	ENG H	217		224	10789	WORK RM	0509
80500	015	0280	ENG H	218		224	10789	WORK RM	0509
80500	015	0285	ENG H	220		391	40150	CONF RM	0503
80500	015	0290	ENG H	221	*	2759	40250	READING	0503
80500	015	0291	ENG H	221	*	1196	40270	STACKS	0502
80500	015	0390	ENG H	319		1006	40270	STACKS	0502
80500	015	0400	ENG H	321		140	40270	STACKS	0502
80500	015	0410	ENG H	323A		12	40270	STACKS	0502
80500	015	0415	ENG H	323B		126	40270	STACKS	0502
80500	015	0420	ENG H	323C		54	40270	STACKS	0502
80500	015	0425	ENG H	323D		54	40270	STACKS	0502
80500	015	0430	ENG H	323E		88	40270	STACKS	0502
80500	015	0435	ENG H	323F		88	40270	STACKS	0502
80500	015	0440	ENG H	323G		80	40270	STACKS	0502
80500	015	0445	ENG H	323H		80	40270	STACKS	0502
80500	015	0450	ENG H	323J		90	40270	STACKS	0502
						7084		STACK AREA	0502
						3150		READING AND STUDY	0503
								CARRELS	0504
						173		SERVICE AREA	0506
						1741		OFFICE SPACE	0509
						12148		BUILDING TOTAL	
80500	023	0343	ILL UN	133		1820	40250	READING	0503

APPENDIX B **107**

I 16 - AUDITORIUM, THEATER, CHAPEL, ASSEMBLY HALL AND CONFERENCE   PAGE   5
       ROOMS NOT USED FOR INSTRUCTION

DEPT. CODE	BLDG. CODE	COS CODE	BLDG. ABBREV.	ROOM NO.	AREA	FACILITY CODE	FACILITY DESCR.	SCHEDULE NUMBER
24800	220	0005	K A M	60	437	70789	WORK RM	0605
24800	220	0030	K A M	64	1040	70789	WORK RM	0605
24800	220	0035	K A M	64A	720	70787	STORAGE	0605
24800	220	0040	K A M	64B	432	70787	STORAGE	0605
24800	220	0045	K A M	66 *	700	70789	WORK RM	0605
24800	220	0046	K A M	66 *	60	10070	OFFICE	0609
24800	220	0050	K A M	66A	204	70787	STORAGE	0605
24800	220	0055	K A M	67	496	70290	EXHIBIT	0605
24800	220	0060	K A M	71	270	70787	STORAGE	0605
24800	220	0065	K A M	73	234	70787	STORAGE	0605
24800	220	0085	K A M	161	140	70781	CLOSET	0605
24800	220	0090	K A M	162	1292	70290	EXHIBIT	0605
24800	220	0095	K A M	162A	1292	70290	EXHIBIT	0605
24800	220	0100	K A M	163	425	10786	RECPTN	0609
24800	220	0105	K A M	163A	63	10787	STORAGE	0609
24800	220	0110	K A M	163B	140	10070	OFFICE	0609
24800	220	0115	K A M	163C	10	10781	CLOSET	0609
24800	220	0120	K A M	164	720	70290	EXHIBIT	0605
24800	220	0125	K A M	166	3744	70290	EXHIBIT	0605
24800	220	0130	K A M	168	396	70785	RECEIVE	0605
24800	220	0135	K A M	169	324	10070	OFFICE	0609
24800	220	0140	K A M	171	391	10150	CONF RM	0609

	AUDIT., THEATER, ASSEMBLY HALL	0603
	CONFERENCE ROOMS NOT FOR INSTR.	0604
12117	EXHIBIT AND MUSEUM	0605
1413	OFFICE SPACE	0609
13530	BUILDING TOTAL	

	AUDIT., THEATER, ASSEMBLY HALL	0603
	CONFERENCE ROOMS NOT FOR INSTR.	0604
12117	EXHIBIT AND MUSEUM	0605
1413	OFFICE SPACE	0609
13530	DEPARTMENT TOTAL	

I 17 - GYM, FIELD HOUSE, AND ARMORY SPACE NOT USED FOR INSTRUCTION								PAGE 2
DEPT. CODE	BLDG. CODE	COS CODE	BLDG. ABBREV.	ROOM NO.	AREA	FACILITY CODE	FACILITY DESCR.	SCHEDULE NUMBER
36119	005	0050	GYM AN	205	5430	70450	SEATING	0700
					5430 BUILDING TOTAL			
36119	021	0100	MO GYM	206	500	70450	SEATING	0700
					500 BUILDING TOTAL			
36119	058	0375	HUFF G	200	2550	70450	SEATING	0700
36119	058	0415	HUFF G	208	2444	70450	SEATING	0700
36119	058	0485	HUFF G	310	7520	70450	SEATING	0700
36119	058	0495	HUFF G	320	7520	70450	SEATING	0700
					20034 BUILDING TOTAL			
					25964 DEPARTMENT TOTAL			

I 18 - HOUSING AREA   PAGE   104

DEPT. CODE	BLDG. CODE	COS CODE	BLDG. ABBREV.	ROOM NO.	AREA	FACILITY CODE	FACILITY DESCR.	SCHEDULE NUMBER
82802	273	1670	TOWNSE	1207	165	50510	STUDY SL	0802
82802	273	1675	TOWNSE	1208	165	50510	STUDY SL	0802
82802	273	1680	TOWNSE	1209	165	50510	STUDY SL	0802
82802	273	1685	TOWNSE	1210	165	50510	STUDY SL	0802
82802	273	1690	TOWNSE	1211	165	50510	STUDY SL	0802
82802	273	1695	TOWNSE	1212	279	50510	STUDY SL	0802
82802	273	1700	TOWNSE	1213	220	50510	STUDY SL	0802
82802	273	1705	TOWNSE	1214	150	50510	STUDY SL	0802
82802	273	1710	TOWNSE	1215	35	50560	TOILET	0802
82802	273	1715	TOWNSE	1216	279	50510	STUDY SL	0802
82802	273	1720	TOWNSE	1217	165	50510	STUDY SL	0802
82802	273	1725	TOWNSE	1218	165	50510	STUDY SL	0802
82802	273	1730	TOWNSE	1219	165	50510	STUDY SL	0802
82802	273	1735	TOWNSE	1220	165	50510	STUDY SL	0802
82802	273	1740	TOWNSE	1221	165	50510	STUDY SL	0802
82802	273	1745	TOWNSE	1222	165	50510	STUDY SL	0802
82802	273	1750	TOWNSE	1223	165	50510	STUDY SL	0802
82802	273	1755	TOWNSE	1224	165	50510	STUDY SL	0802
82802	273	1760	TOWNSE	1225	165	50510	STUDY SL	0802
82802	273	1765	TOWNSE	1226	279	50510	STUDY SL	0802
82802	273	1770	TOWNSE	1228	616	50560	TOILET	0802
82802	273	1775	TOWNSE	1229	15	50787	STORAGE	0802
82802	273	1780	TOWNSE	1230	45	50892	HAIR DRY	0802
82802	273	1785	TOWNSE	1231	96	50930	HSG AUX	0802
						MARRIED STUDENT HOUSING		0H01
					72987	UNMARRIED STUDENT HOUSING		0802
						GROUP DINING FACILITIES		0805
					270	OFFICE SPACE		0809
					73257	BUILDING TOTAL		
82802	274	0005	ILL LB	0004	897	50320	ACTIVITY	0802
82802	274	0010	ILL LB	0005	136	60787	STORAGE	0802
82802	274	0015	ILL LB	0006	136	50930	HSG AUX	0802
82802	274	0020	ILL LB	0007	683	60787	STORAGE	0802
82802	274	0025	ILL LB	0008	1794	50320	ACTIVITY	0802
82802	274	0030	ILL LB	0018	390	60787	STORAGE	0802
82802	274	0035	ILL LB	0105	78	50787	STORAGE	0802
82802	274	0040	ILL LB	0106	1287	50320	ACTIVITY	0802
82802	274	0045	ILL LB	0107	1500	50660	LOUNGE	0802
82802	274	0050	ILL LB	0108	1512	50660	LOUNGE	0802
82802	274	0055	ILL LB	0109	120	10070	OFFICE	0809
82802	274	0060	ILL LB	0110	25	50841	WASH RM	0802
82802	274	0065	ILL LB	0111	66	10787	STORAGE	0809
82802	274	0070	ILL LB	0112	120	10070	OFFICE	0809
82802	274	0075	ILL LB	0114	725	10070	OFFICE	0809
						MARRIED STUDENT HOUSING		0H01
					8438	UNMARRIED STUDENT HOUSING		0802
						GROUP DINING FACILITIES		0805
					1031	OFFICE SPACE		0809
					9469	BUILDING TOTAL		

I 19 - STUDENT SERVICE SPACE - UNION, BOOKSTORE, LOUNGE								PAGE 51
DEPT. CODE	BLDG. CODE	COS CODE	BLDG. ABBREV.	ROOM NO.	AREA	FACILITY CODE	FACILITY DESCR.	SCHEDULE NUMBER
82900	023	1873	ILL UN	492B	35	50560	TOILET	0904
82900	023	1878	ILL UN	493	191	50510	STUDY SL	0904
82900	023	1883	ILL UN	493B	35	50560	TOILET	0904
82900	023	1888	ILL UN	494	268	50510	STUDY SL	0904
82900	023	1893	ILL UN	494B	35	50560	TOILET	0904
82900	023	1898	ILL UN	495	190	50510	STUDY SL	0904
82900	023	1903	ILL UN	495B	35	50560	TOILET	0904
82900	023	1908	ILL UN	496	260	50510	STUDY SL	0904
82900	023	1913	ILL UN	496B	35	50560	TOILET	0904
					42419	DINING AND FOOD PREPARATION		0902
					58367	STUDENT USE		0903
					28393	GUEST ROOMS		0904
						STUDENT SVC IN ACAD BLDGS.		0905
					10265	OFFICE SPACE		0909
					139444	BUILDING TOTAL		
82900	071	0005	ARCADE	2	110	50787	STORAGE	0903
82900	071	0010	ARCADE	2A	44	50787	STORAGE	0903
82900	071	0015	ARCADE	4	336	50787	STORAGE	0903
82900	071	0020	ARCADE	6	336	50787	STORAGE	0903
82900	071	0055	ARCADE	102	4041	50787	STORAGE	0903
82900	071	0160	ARCADE	124	48	10070	OFFICE	0909
82900	071	0180	ARCADE	126	48	10070	OFFICE	0909
82900	071	0185	ARCADE	128	48	10070	OFFICE	0909
82900	071	0195	ARCADE	132	1717	50787	STORAGE	0903
82900	071	0200	ARCADE	132A	48	10070	OFFICE	0909
82900	071	0210	ARCADE	140	840	60787	STORAGE	0903
82900	071	0212	ARCADE	140A	60	60787	STORAGE	0903
82900	071	0245	ARCADE	211 *	1280	50787	STORAGE	0903
82900	071	0246	ARCADE	211 *	40	10070	OFFICE	0909
82900	071	0251	ARCADE	220 ¤	130	50787	STORAGE	0903
82900	071	0255	ARCADE	222	657	50787	STORAGE	0903
						DINING AND FOOD PREPARATION		0902
					9551	STUDENT USE		0903
						GUEST ROOMS		0904
						STUDENT SVC IN ACAD BLDGS.		0905
					232	OFFICE SPACE		0909
					9783	BUILDING TOTAL		
82900	153	0006	WARE 1	103	1600	60787	STORAGE	0903
						DINING AND FOOD PREPARATION		0902
					1600	STUDENT USE		0903
						GUEST ROOMS		0904
						STUDENT SVC IN ACAD BLDGS.		0905
						OFFICE SPACE		0909
					1600	BUILDING TOTAL		

APPENDIX B   111

I 20 - CAMPUS HOSPITAL AND HEALTH SERVICE FACILITIES   PAGE   2

DEPT. CODE	BLDG. CODE	COS CODE	BLDG. ABBREV.	ROOM NO.	AREA	FACILITY CODE	FACILITY DESCR.	SCHEDULE NUMBER
10111	003	0580	MCK HO	197	150	10070	OFFICE	1009
10111	003	0585	MCK HO	198	150	10786	RECPTN	1009
10111	003	0590	MCK HO	199	135	10070	OFFICE	1009
10111	003	0825	MCK HO	261	18	10787	STORAGE	1009
10111	003	0840	MCK HO	264	120	10070	OFFICE	1009
10111	003	0845	MCK HO	265	96	10070	OFFICE	1009
10111	003	0850	MCK HO	269	117	10070	OFFICE	1009
10111	003	0855	MCK HO	270	117	10070	OFFICE	1009
10111	003	0860	MCK HO	271	117	10070	OFFICE	1009
10111	003	0865	MCK HO	272	117	10070	OFFICE	1009
10111	003	0870	MCK HO	273	117	10070	OFFICE	1009
10111	003	0875	MCK HO	274	117	10070	OFFICE	1009
10111	003	0880	MCK HO	275	143	10070	OFFICE	1009
10111	003	0885	MCK HO	276	144	10070	OFFICE	1009
10111	003	0890	MCK HO	277	256	10070	OFFICE	1009
10111	003	0891	MCK HO	277A	18	10841	WASH RM	1009
10111	003	0895	MCK HO	277B	9	10787	STORAGE	1009
10111	003	0901	MCK HO	278	160	10070	OFFICE	1009
10111	003	0905	MCK HO	279	143	10070	OFFICE	1009
10111	003	0910	MCK HO	280	143	10070	OFFICE	1009
10111	003	0915	MCK HO	281	143	10070	OFFICE	1009
10111	003	0920	MCK HO	282	143	10070	OFFICE	1009
10111	003	0925	MCK HO	283	132	10070	OFFICE	1009
10111	003	0930	MCK HO	284	132	10070	OFFICE	1009
10111	003	0935	MCK HO	285	132	10070	OFFICE	1009
10111	003	0940	MCK HO	286	132	10070	OFFICE	1009
10111	003	0945	MCK HO	287	336	10150	CONF RM	1009
10111	003	0950	MCK HO	288	81	10070	OFFICE	1009

	AREA TO HOSPITAL BEDS	1002
3798	AREA TO HEALTH SERVICE	1004
	AREA TO LIVING QUARTERS	1005
7836	AREA TO OFFICE	1009
11634	BUILDING TOTAL	

	AREA TO HOSPITAL BEDS	1002
3798	AREA TO HEALTH SERVICE	1004
	AREA TO LIVING QUARTERS	1005
7836	AREA TO OFFICE	1009
11634	DEPARTMENT TOTAL	

I 21 - BUILDINGS AND GROUNDS MAINTENANCE SPACE

PAGE 8

DEPT. CODE	BLDG. CODE	COS CODE	BLDG. ABBREV.	ROOM NO.	AREA	FACILITY CODE	FACILITY DESCR.	SCHEDULE NUMBER
82050	198	0360	PPSB	140	855	10840	FILE RM	1109
82050	198	0365	PPSB	140A	12	10787	STORAGE	1109
82050	198	0370	PPSB	141	666	10070	OFFICE	1109
82050	198	0375	PPSB	141A	15	10787	STORAGE	1109
82050	198	0380	PPSB	141B	144	10070	OFFICE	1109
82050	198	0385	PPSB	141C	208	10070	OFFICE	1109
82050	198	0390	PPSB	142	384	10070	OFFICE	1109
82050	198	0395	PPSB	143	352	10150	CONF RM	1109
82050	198	0400	PPSB	146	1797	55500	SHOP	1102
82050	198	0405	PPSB	149	408	55500	SHOP	1102
82050	198	0410	PPSB	149A	128	55788	VAULT	1102
82050	198	0415	PPSB	150	6261	55787	STORAGE	1102
82050	198	0420	PPSB	153	3273	55500	SHOP	1102
82050	198	0425	PPSB	153A	132	10070	OFFICE	1109
82050	198	0430	PPSB	153B	165	10070	OFFICE	1109
82050	198	0435	PPSB	154	3904	55500	SHOP	1102
82050	198	0440	PPSB	154A	132	10070	OFFICE	1109
82050	198	0445	PPSB	154B	100	55500	SHOP	1102
82050	198	0450	PPSB	154C	100	55500	SHOP	1102
82050	198	0455	PPSB	155	11559	55787	STORAGE	1103
82050	198	0460	PPSB	155A	120	10070	OFFICE	1109
82050	198	0465	PPSB	155B	285	10840	FILE RM	1109
82050	198	0470	PPSB	155C	120	10070	OFFICE	1109
82050	198	0475	PPSB	155D	672	10070	OFFICE	1109
82050	198	0480	PPSB	157	14720	55787	STORAGE	1103
82050	198	0485	PPSB	159	1691	55500	SHOP	1102
82050	198	0490	PPSB	159A	216	10070	OFFICE	1109
82050	198	0495	PPSB	160	3608	55500	SHOP	1102
82050	198	0500	PPSB	160A	384	55500	SHOP	1102
82050	198	0505	PPSB	160B	80	10070	OFFICE	1109
82050	198	0510	PPSB	162	1663	55500	SHOP	1102
82050	198	0515	PPSB	162A	350	55500	SHOP	1102
82050	198	0520	PPSB	162B	45	10788	VAULT	1109
82050	198	0525	PPSB	162C	100	10070	OFFICE	1109
82050	198	0530	PPSB	163	858	55500	SHOP	1102
82050	198	0535	PPSB	164	1574	55500	SHOP	1102
82050	198	0540	PPSB	164A	150	10070	OFFICE	1109
82050	198	0545	PPSB	165	5844	55500	SHOP	1102
82050	198	0550	PPSB	165A	77	10070	OFFICE	1109
82050	198	0555	PPSB	202A	756	55787	STORAGE	1104
82050	198	0560	PPSB	211D	1176	55787	STORAGE	1104
82050	198	0565	PPSB	253B	429	55787	STORAGE	1104
82050	198	0570	PPSB	260	630	55787	STORAGE	1104
					46388		SERVICE SHOPS	1102
					26279		STOREROOM	1103
					14545		WAREHOUSE	1104
					17982		GARAGE	1105
					17005		OFFICE SPACE TO PHYS. PLANT	1109
					122199		BUILDING TOTAL	
82050	234	0245	AAWHSE	8B	280	60787	STORAGE	1104

I 22 - RESEARCH SPACE

PAGE 53

DEPT. CODE	BLDG. CODE	COS CODE	BLDG. ABBREV.	ROOM NO.	AREA	FACILITY CODE	FACILITY DESCR.	SCHEDULE NUMBER
22340	066	0635	M R L	55	95	30130	LAB	1200
22340	066	1410	M R L	105	390	30130	LAB	1200
22340	066	1415	M R L	106	200	30130	LAB	1200
22340	066	1420	M R L	108	630	30130	LAB	1200
22340	066	1465	M R L	120	410	30130	LAB	1200
22340	066	1485	M R L	129	630	30130	LAB	1200
22340	066	1495	M R L	133	522	30130	LAB	1200
22340	066	1535	M R L	142	420	30130	LAB	1200
22340	066	1595	M R L	147	595	30130	LAB	1200
22340	066	1700	M R L	153	95	30130	LAB	1200
22340	066	1780	M R L	171	580	30130	LAB	1200
22340	066	2300	M R L	210	210	30130	LAB	1200
22340	066	2355	M R L	216	200	30130	LAB	1200
22340	066	2360	M R L	217	187	30130	LAB	1200
22340	066	2500	M R L	248	462	30130	LAB	1200
22340	066	2505	M R L	250	441	30130	LAB	1200
22340	066	3240	M R L	310	380	30130	LAB	1200
22340	066	3465	M R L	359	573	30130	LAB	1200
22340	066	4525	M R L	410	630	30130	LAB	1200
22340	066	4530	M R L	413	376	30130	LAB	1200
22340	066	4535	M R L	414	420	30130	LAB	1200
22340	066	4540	M R L	417	376	30130	LAB	1200
22340	066	4555	M R L	426	605	30130	LAB	1200
22340	066	4565	M R L	433	208	30130	LAB	1200
22340	066	4590	M R L	444	128	30130	LAB	1200
22340	066	4610	M R L	455	95	30130	LAB	1200
22340	066	4615	M R L	458	410	30130	LAB	1200
22340	066	4620	M R L	459	181	30130	LAB	1200
22340	066	4625	M R L	460	390	30130	LAB	1200
22340	066	4630	M R L	464	410	30130	LAB	1200

```
                                    11249 RESEARCH LAB                       1200
                                      231 AUXILIARY SPACE TO RESEARCH        1802
                                          HOSPITAL ROOMS TO RESEARCH         1803
                                          GREENHOUSE SPACE TO RESEARCH       1804
                                          ANIMAL ROOMS TO RESEARCH           1806
                                          ANIMAL STALLS TO RESEARCH          1808
                                    11480 BUILDING TOTAL


                                    11249 RESEARCH LAB                       1200
                                      231 AUXILIARY SPACE TO RESEARCH        1802
                                          HOSPITAL ROOMS TO RESEARCH         1803
                                          GREENHOUSE SPACE TO RESEARCH       1804
                                          ANIMAL ROOMS TO RESEARCH           1806
                                          ANIMAL STALLS TO RESEARCH          1808
                                    11480 DEPARTMENT TOTAL
```

I 23 - LAB SCHOOL SPACE

PAGE 2

DEPT. CODE	BLDG. CODE	COS CODE	BLDG. ABBREV.	ROOM NO.	AREA	FACILITY CODE	FACILITY DESCR.	SCHEDULE NUMBER
20450	061	0260	U H S	314	660	20010	CLASSRM	1300
20450	061	0265	U H S	315	120	30789	WORK RM	1300
20450	061	0270	U H S	401	3902	30330	GYM	1300
20450	061	0275	U H S	402	126	30787	STORAGE	1300
20450	061	0280	U H S	403	196	30787	STORAGE	1300
20450	061	0285	U H S	405	3902	20010	CLASSRM	1300
					22215	GENERAL SPACE		1300
					3797	OFFICE SPACE		1302
					26012	BUILDING TOTAL		
20450	063	0005	UHSGYM	4	335	30784	LOCKER	1300
20450	063	0010	UHSGYM	5	32	30787	STORAGE	1300
20450	063	0015	UHSGYM	6	360	30784	LOCKER	1300
20450	063	0020	UHSGYM	7	21	30787	STORAGE	1300
20450	063	0025	UHSGYM	103	3234	30330	GYM	1300
20450	063	0030	UHSGYM	105	864	30450	SEATING	1300
20450	063	0035	UHSGYM	108	49	30787	STORAGE	1300
20450	063	0040	UHSGYM	109	120	30783	DRESSING	1300
20450	063	0045	UHSGYM	110	24	30781	CLOSET	1300
					5039	GENERAL SPACE		1300
						OFFICE SPACE		1302
					5039	BUILDING TOTAL		
20450	150	0005	1208WS	1	273	10789	WORK RM	1309
20450	150	0015	1208WS	5	391	10789	WORK RM	1309
20450	150	0020	1208WS	6	182	10789	WORK RM	1309
20450	150	0025	1208WS	101	169	10789	WORK RM	1309
20450	150	0030	1208WS	103	450	30130	LAB	1300
20450	150	0034	1208WS	106A	18	30782	DARK RM	1300
20450	150	0039	1208WS	106B	163	30782	DARK RM	1300
20450	150	0055	1208WS	201	169	10070	OFFICE	1309
20450	150	0060	1208WS	201A	4	10781	CLOSET	1309
20450	150	0065	1208WS	202	16	10781	CLOSET	1309
20450	150	0070	1208WS	203	180	10070	OFFICE	1309
20450	150	0075	1208WS	203A	12	10781	CLOSET	1309
20450	150	0080	1208WS	205	132	10070	OFFICE	1309
20450	150	0085	1208WS	205A	15	10781	CLOSET	1309
20450	150	0090	1208WS	208	157	10070	OFFICE	1309
20450	150	0095	1208WS	208A	10	10781	CLOSET	1309
20450	150	0100	1208WS	301	224	10070	OFFICE	1309
20450	150	0105	1208WS	301A	16	10781	CLOSET	1309
20450	150	0110	1208WS	303	120	10070	OFFICE	1309
20450	150	0115	1208WS	308	196	10070	OFFICE	1309
20450	150	0120	1208WS	308A	8	10781	CLOSET	1309
20450	150	0125	1208WS	310	156	10070	OFFICE	1309
20450	150	0130	1208WS	310A	9	10781	CLOSET	1309
					631	GENERAL SPACE		1300
					2439	OFFICE SPACE		1302

I 24 – ATHLETIC ASSOCIATION

PAGE 1

DEPT. CODE	BLDG CODE	COS CODE	BLDG. ABBREV.	ROOM NO.	AREA	FACILITY CODE	FACILITY DESCR.	SCHEDULE NUMBER
82680	005	0021	GYM AN	110 □	119	10070	OFFICE	1409
						GENERAL SPACE		1400
					119	OFFICE SPACE		1409
					119	BUILDING TOTAL		
82680	006	0138	ARMORY	137A	180	30787	STORAGE	1400
					180	GENERAL SPACE		1400
						OFFICE SPACE		1409
					180	BUILDING TOTAL		
82680	014	0005	SKAT R	1	767	30784	LOCKER	1400
82680	014	0010	SKAT R	3	360	30784	LOCKER	1400
82680	014	0015	SKAT R	3A	52	30894	SHOWER	1400
82680	014	0020	SKAT R	5	880	30784	LOCKER	1400
82680	014	0025	SKAT R	5B	140	30894	SHOWER	1400
82680	014	0035	SKAT R	7B	230	30787	STORAGE	1400
82680	014	0040	SKAT R	100	170	10070	OFFICE	1409
82680	014	0045	SKAT R	100A	30	10781	CLOSET	1409
82680	014	0055	SKAT R	105	1924	30783	DRESSING	1400
82680	014	0060	SKAT R	108	180	70640	KITCHEN	1400
82680	014	0065	SKAT R	109	308	70680	CANTEEN	1400
82680	014	0070	SKAT R	110	104	30895	SKATE SH	1400
82680	014	0075	SKAT R	111	645	30781	CLOSET	1400
82680	014	0085	SKAT R	121	100	30891	FIRST AD	1400
82680	014	0090	SKAT R	121A	20	30781	CLOSET	1400
82680	014	0095	SKAT R	121B	33	30781	CLOSET	1400
82680	014	0100	SKAT R	122	200	30787	STORAGE	1400
82680	014	0105	SKAT R	124	12	30891	FIRST AD	1400
82680	014	0110	SKAT R	221	2520	70450	SEATING	1400
82680	014	0115	SKAT R	222	2520	70450	SEATING	1400
					10995	GENERAL SPACE		1400
					200	OFFICE SPACE		1409
					11195	BUILDING TOTAL		
82680	021	0020	MO GYM	109 □	90	30896	TOWEL	1400
82680	021	0025	MO GYM	109A	114	30894	SHOWER	1400
82680	021	0040	MO GYM	113	665	30784	LOCKER	1400
82680	021	0050	MO GYM	115	437	30891	FIRST AD	1400
82680	021	0130	MO GYM	215	642	30784	LOCKER	1400
					1948	GENERAL SPACE		1400
						OFFICE SPACE		1409
					1948	BUILDING TOTAL		
82680	058	0182	HUFF G	93C	400	30784	LOCKER	1400
82680	058	0183	HUFF G	93D	400	30784	LOCKER	1400

I 25 - QUASI-UNIVERSITY GROUPS

PAGE 4

DEPT. CODE	BLDG. CODE	COS CODE	BLDG. ABBREV.	ROOM NO.	AREA	FACILITY CODE	FACILITY DESCR.	SCHEDULE NUMBER
26800	109	1325	N R B	436	336	30725	DISTILL	1500
26800	109	1335	N R B	462	256	30130	LAB	1500
26800	109	1340	N R B	463	300	10070	OFFICE	1509
26800	109	1345	N R B	463A	77	30782	DARK RM	1500
26800	109	1350	N R B	464	150	10070	OFFICE	1509
26800	109	1355	N R B	465	200	30070	OFFICE	1500
26800	109	1375	N R B	469	378	10070	OFFICE	1509
26800	109	1380	N R B	472	860	10787	STORAGE	1509
26800	109	1385	N R B	475	1276	40250	READING	1500
					24246	GENERAL SPACE		1500
					26448	OFFICE SPACE		1509
					50694	BUILDING TOTAL		
26800	128	0005	GEO SL	100	12	30781	CLOSET	1500
26800	128	0010	GEO SL	101	99	10070	OFFICE	1509
26800	128	0015	GEO SL	102	1447	30130	LAB	1500
26800	128	0020	GEO SL	103	128	30787	STORAGE	1500
26800	128	0025	GEO SL	103A	182	30789	WORK RM	1500
26800	128	0030	GEO SL	107	735	30130	LAB	1500
26800	128	0035	GEO SL	110	992	30130	LAB	1500
26800	128	0040	GEO SL	111	450	30130	LAB	1500
26800	128	0045	GEO SL	203	568	30500	SHOP	1500
26800	128	0050	GEO SL	204 *	789	30130	LAB	1500
26800	128	0051	GEO SL	204 *	150	30130	LAB	1500
26800	128	0055	GEO SL	204A	9	30781	CLOSET	1500
26800	128	0065	GEO SL	207	204	30130	LAB	1500
26800	128	0070	GEO SL	209	187	30500	SHOP	1500
26800	128	0075	GEO SL	210	1086	30130	LAB	1500
26800	128	0080	GEO SL	211	357	30130	LAB	1500
26800	128	0085	GEO SL	214	224	10070	OFFICE	1509
26800	128	0090	GEO SL	214A	88	10787	STORAGE	1509
					7296	GENERAL SPACE		1500
					411	OFFICE SPACE		1509
					7707	BUILDING TOTAL		
26800	133	0010	N R G	102	1925	55914	GARAGE	1500
26800	133	0015	N R G	102B	357	55914	GARAGE	1500
26800	133	0025	N R G	103B	2311	55914	GARAGE	1500
26800	133	0030	N R G	202	1335	60787	STORAGE	1500
26800	133	0035	N R G	203	558	60787	STORAGE	1500
					6486	GENERAL SPACE		1500
						OFFICE SPACE		1509
					6486	BUILDING TOTAL		
					38028	GENERAL SPACE		1500
					26859	OFFICE SPACE		1509
					64887	DEPARTMENT TOTAL		

APPENDIX B 117

I 26 - ALL SPACE BEING REMODELED, UNASSIGNED OR TO BE RAZED								PAGE 8
DEPT. CODE	BLDG. CODE	COS CODE	BLDG. ABBREV.	ROOM NO.	AREA	FACILITY CODE	FACILITY DESCR.	SCHEDULE NUMBER
99000	006	0120	ARMORY	133A	44	60787	STORAGE	1602
99000	006	0163	ARMORY	141	280	30500	SHOP	1602
99000	006	0223	ARMORY	155	880	30787	STORAGE	1602
99000	006	0270	ARMORY	186	30	60787	STORAGE	1602
99000	006	0378	ARMORY	222A	272	10070	OFFICE	1602
99000	006	0383	ARMORY	222B	416	10070	OFFICE	1602
99000	006	0490	ARMORY	235J	481	60787	STORAGE	1602
99000	006	0878	ARMORY	327	228	60787	STORAGE	1602
							SPACE BEING REMODELED	1600
						2631	UNASSIGNED SPACE	1602
							PROPERTIES TO BE RAZED	1604
						2631	BUILDING TOTAL	
99000	046	2765	ADM B	464	30	60787	STORAGE	1602
99000	046	2780	ADM B	465	45	60787	STORAGE	1602
99000	046	2830	ADM B	468W	130	60787	STORAGE	1602
99000	046	2845	ADM B	469E	54	60787	STORAGE	1602
							SPACE BEING REMODELED	1600
						259	UNASSIGNED SPACE	1602
							PROPERTIES TO BE RAZED	1604
						259	BUILDING TOTAL	
99000	062	0029	CD LAB	15	2555	60787	STORAGE	1602
							SPACE BEING REMODELED	1600
						2555	UNASSIGNED SPACE	1602
							PROPERTIES TO BE RAZED	1604
						2555	BUILDING TOTAL	
99000	077	0005	SA E L	100	120	30787	STORAGE	1600
99000	077	0010	SA E L	101	266	30130	LAB	1600
99000	077	0015	SA E L	102	450	30796	TANK RM	1600
99000	077	0020	SA E L	102B	120	30130	LAB	1600
99000	077	0025	SA E L	102C	165	30130	LAB	1600
99000	077	0030	SA E L	103	112	30920	PUMP RM	1600
99000	077	0034	SA E L	110 *	504	30500	SHOP	1600
99000	077	0036	SA E L	110 *	1008	30130	LAB	1600
99000	077	0040	SA E L	200	336	30130	LAB	1600
99000	077	0045	SA E L	202A *	133	30130	LAB	1600
99000	077	0046	SA E L	202A *	35	10070	OFFICE	1600
99000	077	0050	SA E L	202D *	278	30130	LAB	1600
99000	077	0051	SA E L	202D *	50	10070	OFFICE	1600
99000	077	0055	SA E L	202E	140	30721	CON TEMP	1600
99000	077	0060	SA E L	300	492	10070	OFFICE	1600
99000	077	0065	SA E L	302	276	30787	STORAGE	1600
99000	077	0070	SA E L	303	120	10070	OFFICE	1600
99000	077	0075	SA E L	304	96	10070	OFFICE	1600
99000	077	0080	SA E L	305	108	30130	LAB	1600

I 27 - WAREHOUSE STORAGE   PAGE 15

DEPT. CODE	BLDG. CODE	COS CODE	BLDG. ABBREV.	ROOM NO.	AREA	FACILITY CODE	FACILITY DESCR.	SCHEDULE NUMBER
05100	046	2530	ADM B	402E	154	60787	STORAGE	1700
05100	046	2540	ADM B	403	76	60787	STORAGE	1700
05100	046	2550	ADM B	403E	99	60787	STORAGE	1700
05100	046	2560	ADM B	404	72	60787	STORAGE	1700
05100	046	2570	ADM B	404E	88	60787	STORAGE	1700
05100	046	2590	ADM B	405	68	60787	STORAGE	1700
05100	046	2600	ADM B	405E	82	60787	STORAGE	1700
05100	046	2610	ADM B	406	76	60787	STORAGE	1700
05100	046	2615	ADM B	406E	99	60787	STORAGE	1700
05100	046	2625	ADM B	407	72	60787	STORAGE	1700
05100	046	2630	ADM B	407E	88	60787	STORAGE	1700
05100	046	2645	ADM B	408E	94	60787	STORAGE	1700
05100	046	2660	ADM B	409E	110	60787	STORAGE	1700

                                                      1178 BUILDING TOTAL

| 05100 | 113 | 0040 | DAV HS | 31 | 450 | 60787 | STORAGE | 1700 |

                                                      450 BUILDING TOTAL

| 05100 | 156 | 0040 | LAW B | 68E | 510 | 60787 | STORAGE | 1700 |

                                                      510 BUILDING TOTAL

                                                      2138 DEPARTMENT TOTAL

I 28 - AUXILIARY LAB SPACE   PAGE   52

DEPT. CODE	BLDG. CODE	COS CODE	BLDG. ABBREV.	ROOM NO.	AREA	FACIL. CODE	FACILITY DESCR.	SCHED. NO.	AUX.TO TCH.	AUX.TO RES.
22530	117	0002	N E L	102A	158	30500	SHOP	1802	42	116
22530	117	0013	N E L	104D	75	30782	DARK RM	1802	20	55
22530	117	0025	N E L	106C	13	30781	CLOSET	1802	3	10
22530	117	0045	N E L	108	89	30787	STORAGE	1802	23	66
22530	117	0135	N E L	156B	768	30130	LAB	1802	538	230
					1103		AUXILIARY SPACE	1802		
							HOSPITAL ROOMS	1803		
							GREENHOUSE SPACE	1804		
							ANIMAL ROOMS	1806		
							ANIMAL STALLS	1808		
					1103		BUILDING TOTAL		626	477
22530	182	0010	NUC RE	5	67	30787	STORAGE	1802	10	57
22530	182	0015	NUC RE	6	26	30894	SHOWER	1802	4	22
22530	182	0025	NUC RE	102 *	146	30722	CONTROL	1802	22	124
22530	182	0028	NUC RE	106	72	30787	STORAGE	1802	11	61
22530	182	0040	NUC RE	201	695	30787	STORAGE	1802	104	591
					1006		AUXILIARY SPACE	1802		
							HOSPITAL ROOMS	1803		
							GREENHOUSE SPACE	1804		
							ANIMAL ROOMS	1806		
							ANIMAL STALLS	1808		
					1006		BUILDING TOTAL		151	855
					2109		AUXILIARY SPACE	1802		
							HOSPITAL ROOMS	1803		
							GREENHOUSE SPACE	1804		
							ANIMAL ROOMS	1806		
							ANIMAL STALLS	1808		
					2109		DEPARTMENT TOTAL		777	1332

I 50 - SUMMARY OF SPACE ASSIGNMENT BY CATEGORY			PAGE	154
36209	P E W			

SCHED. NO.	TYPE OF SPACE	AREA	TOTAL BY CATEGORY	PERCENT OF TOTAL
0200	SCHEDULED LABORATORIES	414		.7
1802	AUXILIARY LABS TO INSTRUCTION	7		
1804	GREENHOUSE SPACE TO INSTRUCTION			
1806	ANIMAL ROOMS TO INSTRUCTION			
1808	ANIMAL STALLS TO INSTRUCTION		421	
0300	GYMS, POOLS AND DRILL HALLS TO INSTRUCTION	32342		51.0
0302	SERVICE TO GYMS, POOLS AND DRILL HALLS	16483	48825	26.0
0401	OFFICE SPACE WITH OCCUPANTS	3985		6.3
0402	WORK CONFERENCE AND FILE ROOMS	145		.2
0403	OFFICE SPACE WITHIN LABORATORIES			
0404	STORAGE, CLOSETS, AND VAULT SPACE	138	4268	.2
0700	GYM, FIELDHOUSE, ARMORY NOT USED FOR INSTR.	4874	4874	7.7
0902	DINING AND KITCHEN IN UNION			
0903	STUDENT SPACE IN UNION AND BOOKSTORE			
0904	GUEST ROOMS IN UNION			
0905	STUDENT SERVICES IN ACADEMIC BLDGS.	2110		3.3
0909	OFFICE SPACE IN UNION BUILDING		2110	
1200	RESEARCH LAB	2906		4.6
1802	AUXILIARY SPACE TO RESEARCH	7		
1804	GREENHOUSE SPACE TO RESEARCH			
1806	ANIMAL ROOMS TO RESEARCH			
1808	ANIMAL STALLS TO RESEARCH		2913	
	GRAND TOTAL		63411	

I 51 - SUMMARY OF SPACE ASSIGNMENT BY BUILDING   PAGE   11

012	NOYES			
SCHED. NO.	TYPE OF SPACE	AREA	TOTAL BY CATEGORY	PERCENT OF TOTAL
0100	SCHEDULED CLASSROOMS	9891		9.0
0102	SERVICE ROOMS TO CLASSROOMS		9891	
0200	SCHEDULED LABORATORIES	11047		10.0
1802	AUXILIARY LABS TO INSTRUCTION	3836		3.5
1804	GREENHOUSE SPACE TO INSTRUCTION			
1806	ANIMAL ROOMS TO INSTRUCTION			
1808	ANIMAL STALLS TO INSTRUCTION		14883	
0401	OFFICE SPACE WITH OCCUPANTS	13840		12.6
0402	WORK CONFERENCE AND FILE ROOMS	1200		1.1
0403	OFFICE SPACE WITHIN LABORATORIES	11295		10.3
0404	STORAGE, CLOSETS, AND VAULT SPACE	236	26571	.2
0502	STACK AREA TO LIBRARY	2575		2.3
0503	READING AND STUDY AREA TO LIBRARY	2001		1.8
0504	CARREL SPACE TO LIBRARY			
0506	SERVICE AREA TO LIBRARY			
0509	OFFICE AREA TO LIBRARY	150	4726	.1
1200	RESEARCH LAB	39960		36.3
1802	AUXILIARY SPACE TO RESEARCH	7261		6.6
1804	GREENHOUSE SPACE TO RESEARCH			
1806	ANIMAL ROOMS TO RESEARCH			
1808	ANIMAL STALLS TO RESEARCH		47221	
1700	WAREHOUSE STORAGE	6666	6666	6.1
	GRAND TOTAL		109958	

APPENDIX C

Date:_____

TO: Executive Vice-President and Provost
Copies after
approval to: Vice-President and Comptroller
Director Physical Plant
Associate Director Physical Plant
Director Campus Planning
University Architect
Superintendent of Buildings and Grounds
SUBJECT: Proposed Foreign Languages Building

This letter is written to request permission to prepare a Program Statement for a Foreign Languages Building for the language departments of the College of Liberal Arts and Sciences.

A. The total area of the building is to be 67,010 net assignable square feet. The area generated for each academic department using the "Numeric Method" is shown below:

Department	Office	Research	Storage	Classroom	Other	Total
French	10,362	569	109			11,040
Slavic Lang. and Lit.	3,624	210	38			3,872
Span., Ital., and Port.	8,269	576	89			8,934
Linguistics	2,739	223	29			2,991
Germanic Lang. and Lit.	7,376	266	76			7,718
Classics	3,005	130	31			3,166
English as a Second Lang.	2,311	54	24			2,389
LAS Admin.					11,500[a]	11,500
LAS Teach. Asst.	1,800					1,800
Gen. Univ.				12,600	1,000[b]	13,600
Total Sq. Ft.	39,486	2,028	396	12,600	12,500	67,010

[a] Language laboratory for French, Spanish, Italian, Portuguese, and German.
[b] Commons or student lounge space.

B. These calculations are based upon the following enrollments projected in 19XX:

Department	FS	JS	FTE Beg. Grad.	FTE Adv. Grad.	Total	Headcount Beg. Grad.	Headcount Adv. Grad.
French	385	236	82	108	811	53	51
Slavic Lang. and Lit.	45	53	61	112	271	29	17
Span., Ital., and Port.	307	175	38	35	555	49	58
Linguistics	1	9	13	22	45	18	23
Germanic Lang. and Lit.	285	200	63	118	666	43	17
Classics	67	105	4	8	184	8	12
English as a Second Lang.	6	7	18	...	31	25	..
Total	1,096	785	279	403	2,563	225	178

C. The staff in 19XX were estimated to be:

	Teaching	Research Less RA[a]	Total Requiring Office Space
French	68.14	.59	76.74
Slavic Lang. and Lit.	15.90	1.99	25.36
Span., Ital., and Port.	43.62	.29	61.25
Linguistics	8.68	1.32	20.29
Germanic Lang. and Lit.	49.32	....	54.64
Classics	14.90	.75	22.26
English as a Second Lang.	11.17	....	17.12
Total	211.73	4.94	277.66

[a] Research Assistant.

D. The existing space presently assigned to the following departments will be vacated for reassignment to other units on the campus after completion of the proposed building.

By Department		By Building	
French	6,638	Building No. 111	1,425
Slavic Lang. and Lit.	2,413	Building No. 112	20,312
Span., Ital., and Port.	5,895	Building No. 113	3,163
Linguistics	1,587	Building No. 114	712
Germanic Lang. and Lit.	4,490	Building No. 115	1,100
Classics	1,974	Building No. 116	1,587
LAS Admin.	8,595	Building No. 117	1,648
		Building No. 118	1,645
Total	31,592	Total	31,592

NOTE: In this case, all existing space is to be vacated. If a portion of the existing space were to be retained, the space would be listed or a reference to a letter of agreement would be cited.

E. Based on current costs of similar facilities, it is estimated that this project will cost approximately $_____. Firm cost estimates will be developed at the time the Program Statement is prepared.

It is further understood that the approval to write a Program Statement does not constitute a commitment that this project will be included in the 19XX-XX Capital Budget Request. Although this project has been approved by the College of Liberal Arts and Sciences Building Committee, and placed in priority one, it is understood that this project must be reviewed by the Campus Planning Committee before being considered by the Building Program Committee for possible inclusion in the 19XX-XX Capital Budget Request.

Project Coordinator_____

Head of Department_____

Dean of College_____

Planning Officer_____

APPENDIX D

PROGRAM STATEMENT

Foreign Languages Building
University of Illinois
Urbana, Illinois

Compiled by Planning Office

The following Program Statement for the Foreign Languages Building has been reviewed and is accepted as a basis for preparing preliminary drawings for this project.

Building Program Chairman_____

Dean of College_____

Planning Office_____

Office of the Campus Architect_____

PROGRAM STATEMENT
FOREIGN LANGUAGES BUILDING
University of Illinois
Urbana-Champaign Campus

The Foreign Languages Building is intended to create new and expanded office facilities for the following academic units:

Department:
  Classics
  French
  Germanic Languages and Literature
  Linguistics
  Spanish, Italian, and Portuguese
  Slavic Languages and Literature
Division:
  English as a Second Language

In addition to providing office space for the above academic units, this project is intended to provide classroom and language laboratory facilities that are centrally located. The size and number of classrooms included in this project are planned to meet the classroom needs of the total campus, plus partially meet the needs of the academic units housed in the building.

The language laboratory serves as an instructional tool for the Foreign Languages, Classics, and Linguistics Departments, and to the Division of English as a Second Language. It does this by providing the following:

1. A collection of foreign language instructional audio and visual programs.
2. A library of foreign language instructional films, transparencies, and slides.
3. Facilities for producing the above audio and visual aids, where satisfactory commercial materials are unavailable.
4. A pool of portable audio and visual equipment for use in language instruction.
5. Computer-based multimedia instructional facilities for the student to use either as a member of a class, or as an individual.
6. Facilities for advanced research in phonetics.

The total area of 12,750 square feet allocated for the language laboratory provides 8,400 square feet for student stations; 1,080 square feet for remote-control equipment and program storage; 2,070 square feet for production and repair; 360 square feet for phonetic research; and 840 square feet of administrative office area.

GENERAL CONSIDERATIONS

Purpose of the Program Statement. The purpose of this Program Statement is to provide a basis for preparing preliminary drawings by the project architect. It should be regarded as a goal for arriving at an acceptable set of preliminary drawings. This statement sets forth the general facilities requested. Specific details are to be worked out in conferences with the University of Illinois staff.

Site. The area bounded by Mathews Avenue on the east, Smith Memorial Hall on the south, the Quadrangle on the west, and Davenport Hall on the north.

Site Clearance. The Agronomy Annex and Greenhouses and the State Natural History Survey Building will be demolished and the activities in these facilities well be relocated.

Site Restrictions:
1. Certain trees on the site are to remain.
2. The perimeter of the building above ground should not extend (a) into the Quadrangle farther than the west edge of Davenport Hall; (b) farther to the east than Smith Memorial Hall; and (c) farther south than the south line of Lincoln Hall.
3. The height of the building must not exceed that of Smith Memorial Hall.

Traffic Pattern. The heavy flow of student traffic to the classroom and language laboratory areas should be isolated from that to the office areas.

Elevator. Elevator service will be provided.

Temperature Control. This facility will be completely air conditioned.

Sun Control. Protection from the sun will be necessary where large expanses of glass are involved.

Provisions for Wheel Chairs. Provisions must be made for users of wheel chairs.

Bell System. A bell system to indicate class changes should be provided in the classroom and language laboratory areas.

Windows. It is highly desirable to have windows in all offices.

Electrical. Only special electrical requirements will be indicated.

Telephones. All office areas will be provided with telephone service.

Drinking Fountains. All drinking fountains shall be of the refrigerated type.

Building Directory. Major entrances should be provided with a glass-enclosed directory.

Receiving Entrance. A delivery entrance for supplies must be provided. This need not be a separate entrance.

Financial Assistance. It is contemplated that an application will be prepared for Title I funds of the Higher Education Facilities Act. Specific application requirements will have to be met. Details to be furnished at a later date.

Lighting in the Language Laboratory Area. Study must be given to the type of lighting to be used in this area, as certain types, such as fluorescent, may affect the functioning of the equipment.

Noise Control in the Language Laboratory Area. Acoustical treatment will be necessary to reduce disturbances, as the equipment used in this area is sensitive to noise.

Duct System in the Language Laboratory Area. An under-floor duct distribution system must be developed for the wiring for the audio-visual equipment; also for the power distribution system. It must be stressed that the type of distribution system designed for both must be flexible to permit the locating of audio-visual stations anywhere in the room. The reason for this degree of flexibility is that the equipment to be installed in this building will be replaced because of advances in technology during the life of the building. Flexibility is needed to the extent provided by a raised-floor system in a typical computer installation.

Expansion of Language Laboratory Facilities. Future expansion of the language laboratory facilities is to be into the classroom area; therefore, the classroom-type language laboratory, as planned, is equal to two 420-square-foot classrooms, and the library-type language laboratory is equal to four 420-square-foot classrooms.

Language Laboratory Equipment. The PLATO (Programmed Logic for Automatic Teaching Operations) video system under development by the Computer-Based Education Research Laboratory will be used for all student stations and at specified locations throughout the language laboratory area. Accessory to and electronically controlled by the PLATO equipment will be time-shared Audio Program and individual Audio Record units. These must be compatible with the PLATO system. The other equipment listed for this area is what is thought to be required in terms of availability of present-day equipment. It should be recognized that technology is advancing quite rapidly in this area; therefore, more advanced equipment may be available by the time specific equipment must be selected. Detailed equipment specifications to be furnished at a later date.

Public Telephones. Provisions should be made for at least one public pay telephone, preferably in a public area near the lounge.

Size of Office. The office sizes as stated in this Program Statement are to be considered maximum, as it is more important to maintain the number of offices than it is to have fewer offices of a larger size.

Building Efficiency. This building was programmed on the basis that the net assignable square feet (NASF) total 60 per cent of the gross square feet. This is the minimum building efficiency currently considered by the Illinois Board of Higher Education. Drawings which indicate a building efficiency of less than 60 per cent will be reviewed on the basis of a breakdown of the following nonassignable categories: mechanical, circulation, restroom, custodial, and construction.

Mail Distribution. Each departmental office must be provided with mail boxes that can be stuffed from within the departmental offices which will enable the faculty to get their mail from the corridor side from a locked mail box. The number of mail boxes for each department is to be determined at a later date.

Programmed Areas. The Central Office on the Use of Space will be furnished a schedule of the programmed and the proposed net assignable square feet at each stage of the planning.

Proposed Alternate to Reduce Scope of the Project. To avoid delays in starting this project because of the possibility of bids exceeding the project budget, it is proposed that the following areas be included as an alternate:

Classrooms (12 @ 420)	5,040
Faculty-Student Meeting Room	1,000
Total net assignable square feet	6,040

Estimated Project Timetable:

	Month	Year
Complete HEFA Title I Application		
Final Design Approval		
Complete Working Drawings		
Start Construction		
Complete Construction		

Cost Analysis:

	Amount
Project Budget	
Construction Budget	
Project Cost per Gross Square Foot	
Construction Cost per Gross Square Foot	

SPECIFIC CONSIDERATIONS

Summary of Space

Area Code	Description of Room	Net Assignable Square Feet (NASF)	
A	*General Area*		
A-1	Classrooms 18 @ 420	7,560	
A-2	Seminar Rooms 12 @ 280	3,360	
A-3	Phonetics Classroom	420	
A-4	Observation Room	420	
A-5	Faculty-Student Meeting Room	1,000	
A-6	Central Duplicating	400	
A-7	Assistants' Offices 7 @ 120	840	
	Subtotal — General		14,000
B	*Classics Office Area*		
B-1	Department Office	240	
B-2	Department Head	180	
B-3	Administrative Offices 2 @ 120	240	
B-4	Secretarial Office	120	
B-5	Conference Room	180	
B-6	Library	240	
B-7	Supply Storage and Workroom	120	
B-8	Faculty Offices 12 @ 120	1,440	
B-9	Assistants' Offices 4 @ 120	480	
	Subtotal — Classics		3,240
C	*French Office Area*		
C-1	Department Office	240	
C-2	Department Head	180	
C-3	Administrative Offices 4 @ 120	480	

Summary of Space — (Continued)

Area Code	Description of Room	Net Assignable Square Feet (NASF)	
C-4	Secretarial Offices 3 @ 120	360	
C-5	Conference — Library Room	480	
C-6	Workroom	120	
C-7	Student Reading and Waiting Room	180	
C-8	Division Office (Comparative Lit.)	180	
C-9	Secretarial Office (Comparative Lit.)	120	
C-10	Faculty Offices 33 @ 120	3,960	
C-11	Assistants' Offices 40 @ 120	4,800	
	Subtotal — French		11,100
D	*Germanic Languages and Literature Office Area*		
D-1	Department Reception Office	120	
D-2	Department Clerical Office	360	
D-3	Department Head	180	
D-4	Executive Secretary's Office	120	
D-5	Department Head Secretary's Office	120	
D-6	Supply Storage and Workroom	120	
D-7	Conference Rooms 2 @ 240	480	
D-8	Secretarial Offices 2 @ 120	240	
D-9	Administrative Offices 2 @ 120	240	
D-10	Faculty Offices 48 @ 120	5,760	
	Subtotal — German		7,740
E	*Linguistics Office Area*		
E-1	Department Office	240	
E-2	Department Head	180	
E-3	Administrative Office	120	
E-4	Conference Room	240	
E-5	Workroom	120	
E-6	Supply Storage	60	
E-7	Faculty Offices 13 @ 120	1,560	
E-8	Assistants' Offices 4 @ 120	480	
	Subtotal — Linguistics		3,000
F	*Slavic Languages and Literature Office Area*		
F-1	Department Office	240	
F-2	Department Head	180	
F-3	Secretarial Office	120	
F-4	Conference Room	240	
F-5	Research — Library Room	180	
F-6	Supply Storage and Workroom	120	
F-7	Faculty Offices 15 @ 120	1,800	
F-8	Assistants' Offices 8 @ 120	960	
	Subtotal — Slavic		3,840
G	*Spanish, Italian, and Portuguese Office Area*		
G-1	Department Office	360	
G-2	Department Head	180	
G-3	Administrative Offices 2 @ 120	240	
G-4	Staff Offices 2 @ 120	240	
G-5	Conference Room	480	
G-6	Supply Storage	120	
G-7	Workroom	120	
G-8	Faculty Offices 26 @ 120	3,120	
G-9	Assistants' Offices 34 @ 120	4,080	
	Subtotal — Spanish		8,940

Summary of Space — (Continued)

Area Code	Description of Room	Net Assignable Square Feet (NASF)	
H	*English as a Second Language Office Area*		
H-1	Division Office	240	
H-2	Director's Office	180	
H-3	Conference Room	240	
H-4	Research Room	180	
H-5	Supply Storage and Workroom	120	
H-6	Faculty Offices 12 @ 120	1,440	
	Subtotal — English		2,400
J	*Language Lab Area*		
J-1	Phonetics Laboratory	360	
J-2	Shop	480	
J-3	Control Room	240	
J-4	Tape Production	540	
J-5	Audio Teaching Equipment	360	
J-6	Visual Teaching Equipment	450	
J-7	Remote Equipment Rooms 2 @ 360	720	
J-8	Program Storage 2 @ 180	360	
J-9	Library-type Language Labs 2 @ 1,680	3,360	
J-10	Classroom-type Language Labs 6 @ 840	5,040	
J-11	Director's Office	180	
J-12	Assistant Director's Office	120	
J-13	Secretary and Reception	240	
J-14	Program Coordinator's Offices 2 @ 90	180	
J-15	Staff Lounge	120	
	Subtotal — Language Labs		12,750
	Total Net Assignable Square Feet		67,010
	Nonassignable area (mechanical, restrooms, entrances, circulation, exterior walls and interior partitions)		44,673
	Total Gross Area		111,683

"Building Block" Summary

Classrooms	12,120
Instructional Laboratories	11,550
Offices	40,060
Research	2,280
Commons	1,000
Total net assignable square feet	67,010

**Functional Relationship Chart
General Area**

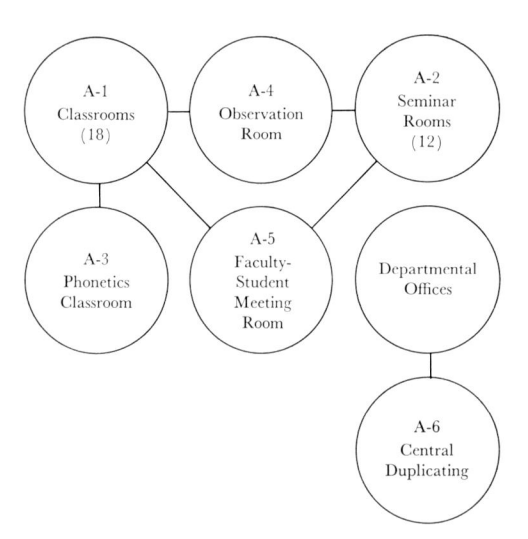

- A-1 Classrooms (18)
- A-4 Observation Room
- A-2 Seminar Rooms (12)
- A-3 Phonetics Classroom
- A-5 Faculty-Student Meeting Room
- Departmental Offices
- A-6 Central Duplicating

**Functional Relationship Chart
Departmental**

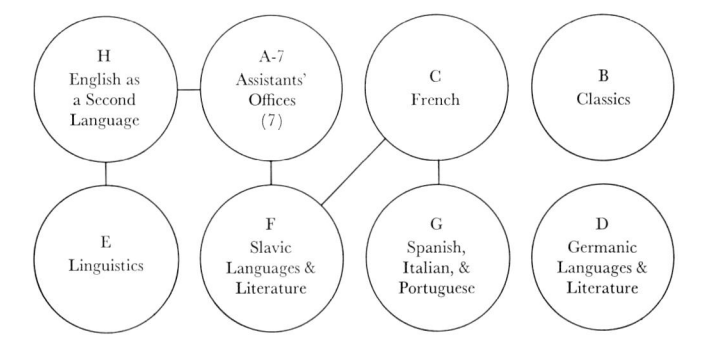

- H English as a Second Language
- A-7 Assistants' Offices (7)
- C French
- B Classics
- E Linguistics
- F Slavic Languages & Literature
- G Spanish, Italian, & Portuguese
- D Germanic Languages & Literature

Functional Relationship Chart
Classics

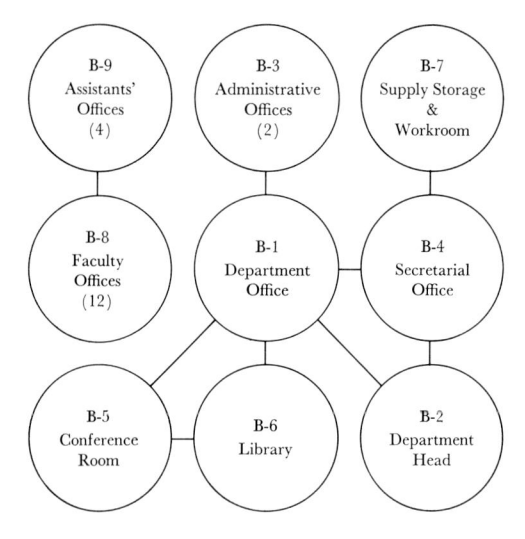

- B-9 Assistants' Offices (4)
- B-3 Administrative Offices (2)
- B-7 Supply Storage & Workroom
- B-8 Faculty Offices (12)
- B-1 Department Office
- B-4 Secretarial Office
- B-5 Conference Room
- B-6 Library
- B-2 Department Head

Functional Relationship Chart
French

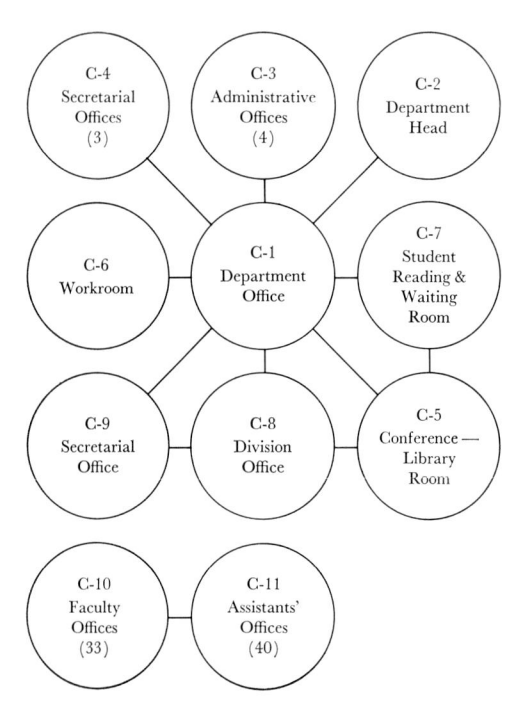

- C-4 Secretarial Offices (3)
- C-3 Administrative Offices (4)
- C-2 Department Head
- C-6 Workroom
- C-1 Department Office
- C-7 Student Reading & Waiting Room
- C-9 Secretarial Office
- C-8 Division Office
- C-5 Conference — Library Room
- C-10 Faculty Offices (33)
- C-11 Assistants' Offices (40)

APPENDIX D 135

Functional Relationship Chart
German

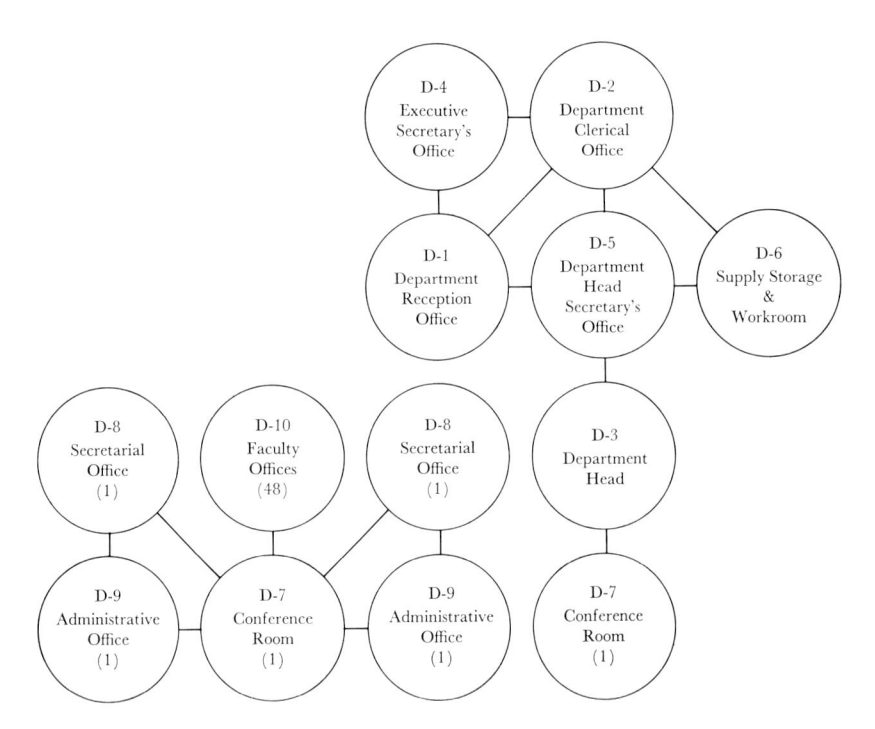

- D-4 Executive Secretary's Office
- D-2 Department Clerical Office
- D-1 Department Reception Office
- D-5 Department Head Secretary's Office
- D-6 Supply Storage & Workroom
- D-8 Secretarial Office (1)
- D-10 Faculty Offices (48)
- D-8 Secretarial Office (1)
- D-3 Department Head
- D-9 Administrative Office (1)
- D-7 Conference Room (1)
- D-9 Administrative Office (1)
- D-7 Conference Room (1)

Functional Relationship Chart
Linguistics

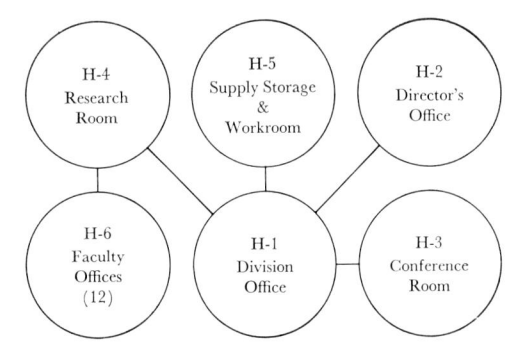

- H-4 Research Room
- H-5 Supply Storage & Workroom
- H-2 Director's Office
- H-6 Faculty Offices (12)
- H-1 Division Office
- H-3 Conference Room

Functional Relationship Chart
Slavic

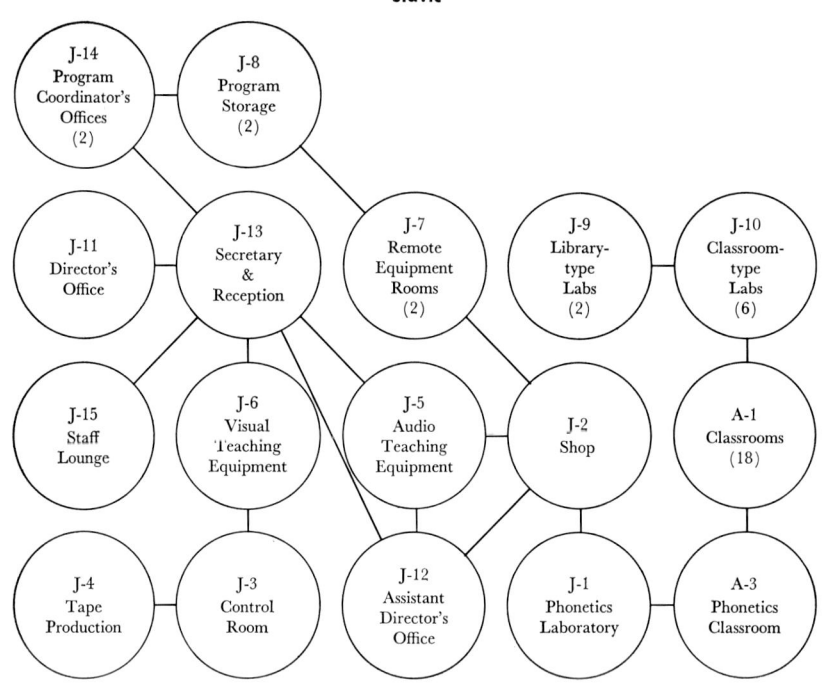

- J-14 Program Coordinator's Offices (2)
- J-8 Program Storage (2)
- J-11 Director's Office
- J-13 Secretary & Reception
- J-7 Remote Equipment Rooms (2)
- J-9 Library-type Labs (2)
- J-10 Classroom-type Labs (6)
- J-15 Staff Lounge
- J-6 Visual Teaching Equipment
- J-5 Audio Teaching Equipment
- J-2 Shop
- A-1 Classrooms (18)
- J-4 Tape Production
- J-3 Control Room
- J-12 Assistant Director's Office
- J-1 Phonetics Laboratory
- A-3 Phonetics Classroom

Functional Relationship Chart
Spanish

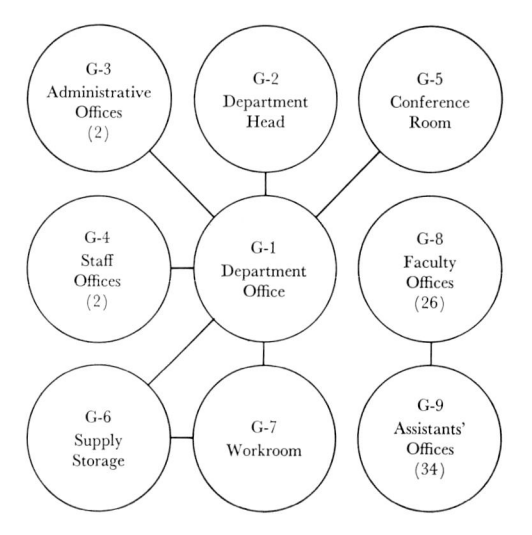

- G-3 Administrative Offices (2)
- G-2 Department Head
- G-5 Conference Room
- G-4 Staff Offices (2)
- G-1 Department Office
- G-8 Faculty Offices (26)
- G-6 Supply Storage
- G-7 Workroom
- G-9 Assistants' Offices (34)

APPENDIX D   **137**

Functional Relationship Chart
English as a Second Language

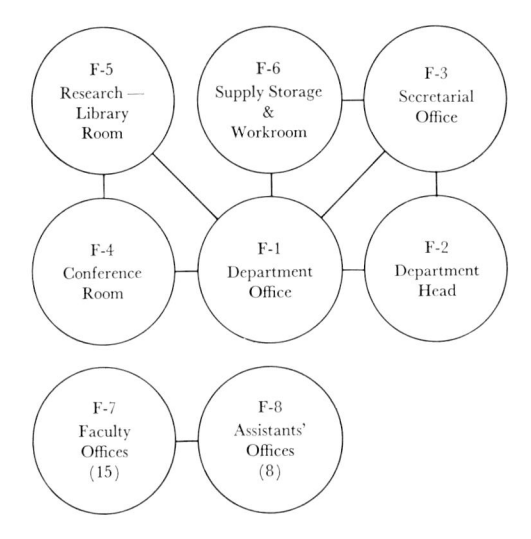

- F-5 Research — Library Room
- F-6 Supply Storage & Workroom
- F-3 Secretarial Office
- F-4 Conference Room
- F-1 Department Office
- F-2 Department Head
- F-7 Faculty Offices (15)
- F-8 Assistants' Offices (8)

Functional Relationship Chart
Language Laboratory Area

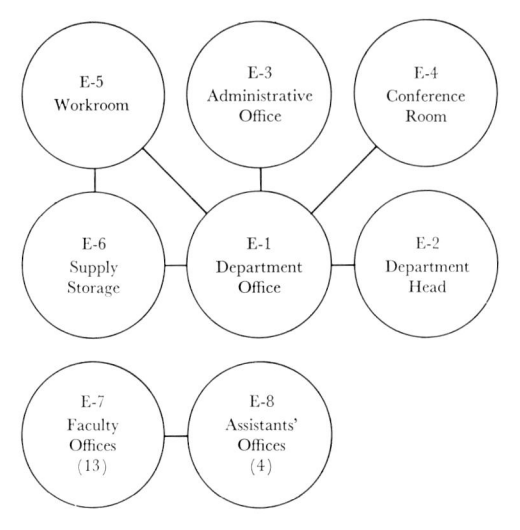

- E-5 Workroom
- E-3 Administrative Office
- E-4 Conference Room
- E-6 Supply Storage
- E-1 Department Office
- E-2 Department Head
- E-7 Faculty Offices (13)
- E-8 Assistants' Offices (4)

Description of Specific Requirements

Area Code	Description of Space	Net Assignable Sq. Ft.	Remarks
A-1	Classrooms (18)	420 Each 7,560 Total	Each room is to contain: Thirty movable tablet-arm chairs; chalkboard across front of room and on one side; 31 coat hooks; desk and chair for instructor; fixed screen adaptable for front end and overhead projection; provision for closed-circuit television connected with campus-wide TV system. This classroom area is to serve as an expansion area for the language laboratories; therefore, a method of extending the electrical duct system will have to be considered.
A-2	Seminar Rooms (12)	280 Each 3,360 Total	Each room is to contain: Seating for 15 people at a table(s) and chairs arrangement; 15 coat hooks; chalkboard at one end.
A-3	Phonetics Classroom	420	This classroom is to be equipped similarly to the regular classrooms (A-1) except this room will be adjacent to the phonetics laboratory (J-1). The equipment listed in this laboratory (J-1) will be used as instructional aids and research in the classroom. The aisles between the student stations must be wide enough to permit rolling carts to move the equipment. Approximately 25 tablet-arm chairs are to be provided. More than the normal number of electrical outlets are required for the operation of the equipment to be used.
A-4	Observation Room	420	This room is to be placed between a classroom and a seminar room. It is to accommodate 30 people. The seating arrangement must be designed so that: (1) 30 people can observe into either the classroom or the seminar room; (2) 20 people can observe into the classroom and ten people into the seminar room; a movable partition must be provided to separate the areas when this room is used as two observation rooms. One-way glass is to be provided on each side of the room. Observers must be capable of hearing the classroom and seminar room discussions; also, when the room is divided, the observation and discussions on one side must not disturb the observation and discussions on the other side. Provisions are to be made in the observation room for filming and taping the classes in the classroom and seminar room.
A-5	Faculty-Student Meeting Room	1,000	Included should be soft furniture to seat 30 people; 40 folding or stacking chairs; folding conference-type tables; provisions for hanging coats and hats for approximately 70 people; base cabinet with sink and wall-hung cabinets above for serving coffee; door must

Description of Specific Requirements — (Continued)

Area Code	Description of Space	Net Assignable Sq. Ft.	Remarks
			be provided to close off from lounge area; and movable partition to divide room. This area should be a separate room and not incorporated with the circulation space.
A-6	Central Duplicating	400	This room should be furnished with a counter on one wall with storage shelving below; table(s); provisions to include such equipment as a small offset press, Getstetner machine, Xerox 2400, collator, and other duplicating equipment.
	Office Areas		
A-7	Assistants' Offices (7)	840	Each office area will contain the usual office furniture such as a desk and chair, side chairs, and in some instances a table and filing cabinet(s). All private offices should be provided with adjustable shelving standards on one side wall. The telephone outlet in each faculty office or assistant's office must be positioned for the use of either one or two users.
B-1	Department Office	240	
B-2	Department Head	180	
B-3	Administrative Offices (2)	240	
B-4	Secretarial Office	120	
B-8	Faculty Offices (12)	1,440	
B-9	Assistants' Offices (4)	480	
C-1	Department Office	240	
C-2	Department Head	180	
C-3	Administrative Offices (4)	480	
C-4	Secretarial Offices (3)	360	
C-8	Division Office	180	
C-9	Secretarial Office	120	
C-10	Faculty Offices (33)	3,960	
C-11	Assistants' Offices (40)	4,800	
D-1	Department Reception Office	120	
D-2	Department Clerical Office	360	
D-3	Department Head	180	
D-4	Executive Secretary's Ofc.	120	
D-5	Dept. Head Secretary's Office	120	
D-8	Secretarial Offices (2)	240	
D-9	Administrative Offices (2)	240	
D-10	Faculty Offices (48)	5,760	
E-1	Department Office	240	
E-2	Department Head	180	
E-3	Administrative Office	120	
E-7	Faculty Offices (13)	1,560	
E-8	Assistants' Offices (4)	480	
F-1	Department Office	240	
F-2	Department Head	180	
F-3	Secretarial Office	120	
F-7	Faculty Offices (15)	1,800	
F-8	Assistants' Offices (8)	960	
G-1	Department Office	360	
G-2	Department Head	180	
G-3	Administrative Offices (2)	240	
G-4	Staff Offices (2)	240	
G-8	Faculty Offices (26)	3,120	
G-9	Assistants' Offices (34)	4,080	
H-1	Division Office	240	
H-2	Director's Office	180	
H-6	Faculty Offices (12)	1,440	

Description of Specific Requirements — (Continued)

Area Code	Description of Space	Net Assignable Sq. Ft.	Remarks
	Supply Storage and Workroom Areas		
B-7	Supply Storage and Workroom	120	Supply storage rooms will be used for the storage of office supplies. Adjustable shelving approximately 12 inches deep should be provided on all walls.
C-6	Workroom	120	
D-6	Supply Storage and Workroom	120	
E-5	Workroom	120	
E-6	Supply Storage	60	
F-6	Supply Storage and Workroom	120	Workrooms will be used by the clerical staff for the assembling of instructional material. They will contain small table(s) or desks, storage and file cabinets.
G-6	Supply Storage	120	
G-7	Workroom	120	
H-5	Supply Storage and Workroom	120	
B-5	Conference Room	180	Ten chairs and a table(s) should be provided; also, a chalkboard at one end of the room.
B-6	Library	240	Adjustable shelving from floor to ceiling should be provided on all wall surfaces. The furniture in this room will include a table plus seating for approximately ten people.
C-5	Conference—Library	480	Adjustable shelving should be provided on three wall surfaces; also, seating at a table(s) for 18 people. Chalkboard at one end.
C-7	Student Reading and Waiting Room	180	This room should be provided with adjustable shelving on at least two walls, plus seating for approximately ten people.
D-7	Conference Rooms (2)	240 Each	Seating for 12 people at a table(s) should be provided; also, a chalkboard at one end of the room.
E-4	Conference Room	240	
F-4	Conference Room	240 Total 960	
F-5	Research—Library Room	180	Seating for eight people plus adjustable shelving on all wall surfaces should be provided.
G-5	Conference Room	480	Seating for 25 people at a table(s) arrangement plus seating for approximately six in lounge-type furniture should be provided; also, a chalkboard at one end of the room.
H-3	Conference Room	240	Seating for 12 people at a table(s) arrangement is to be provided, plus a chalkboard at one end.
H-4	Research Room	180	This room is to provide (1) adequate storage for written and taped materials in built-in wall cabinets, part with locker compartments and part with adjustable shelves; (2) bulletin board, 4′ x 8′; (3) movable equipment will include filing cabinets, work

Description of Specific Requirements — (Continued)

Area Code	Description of Space	Net Assignable Sq. Ft.	Remarks
			table and chairs; bookcase and experimental research equipment to be determined at a later date.

J-1	Phonetics Laboratory	360	This laboratory-workroom will serve the instructional and research needs of several language departments. The following is needed:
			1. Wall counter on which to place equipment, 30″ wide.
			2. Storage wall with adjustable shelving and locking doors.
			3. Table(s) and chairs in center of room.
			4. Equipment to be operated in this room and the phonetics classroom is as follows:
			  a. Two tape recorders with remote-control mechanism.
			  b. Five pairs of tape repeaters.
			  c. Two microphones; one capable of being used as a throat microphone.
			  d. Laryngoscope
			  e. Palathograph
			  f. Sonograph (sound spectrograph)
			  g. Oscillomink
			  h. Oscilloscope
			  i. Pitch meter
			  j. Portable speech synthesizer

J-2	Shop	480	This area will serve as a repair and maintenance center for the language laboratory facilities. It must be sound-treated to minimize transmission of sound to surrounding areas. It will be occupied by two to four people who will be constructing, modifying, and repairing equipment. This shop is to be provided with: 1. Two electrical boxes on each wall with four outlets in each box; one set of two hot at all times, and the other set of two on a master control switch. Each circuit is to be capable of 30 amps. 2. Work bench — 20′ long x 3′ wide. 3. Shelving above work bench with the following equipment located on it: audio generator, condenser checker, phazer null-meter, vacuum tube volt-meter, precision oscilloscope, audio analyzer, tube checker, and transistor checker. 4. Shelving on all other walls. 5. Equipment to be included: drill press; box and pan brake; 36″ shear; notcher and punch press; bench saw; grinder; air compressor; vacuum cleaner; tool cabinet on wheels; four chairs, work bench height; and telephone.

Description of Specific Requirements — (Continued)

Area Code	Description of Space	Net Assignable Sq. Ft.	Remarks
J-3	Control Room	240	This room will be used for both audio and video recording. In this room will be a console containing audio and video switches and fading equipment. All video monitors will be housed in the console itself. There will be a small film island consisting of a slide projector and two moving picture projectors. Rheostat control lighting and an acoustically treated window to the tape production room will be necessary. The console is to be placed in the center of the room, with the film island to the left side of it. Additional space for equipment will be located in a rack placed away from the wall and near the film island.
J-4	Tape Production	540	This room will be used for audio and video taping of small groups and for teacher-training. It is to be equipped with: 1. A small lighting board along with dimmers to operate the special ceiling lights. 2. Microphone outlets to be located below the control room window, and two more to be located on the other walls at a height of 8″ from the floor. 3. Announcer booth which will contain a light, a monitor, a desktop, a microphone, and a chair. 4. Room for at least two small sets with ample room for the film or video camera to move about. 5. Movable equipment will include: large table, six chairs, two cameras — one film and one video, 21 folding chairs.

J-5	Audio Teaching Equipment	360	This room is to serve as an audio recording room. It is to contain the following:
			1. Shelving for portable audio equipment, blank tapes, and storage boxes.
			2. Two racks for remote equipment.
			3. One tape shelf.
			4. One tape duplicator.
			5. One work table 4′ x 6′ in center of room.
			6. Electrical outlets and lights on master switch system by all doors.
			7. Two clocks.
			8. Six tape splicers.
			9. Four recording and editing booths, each with the following specifications:
			  a. Each carrel must be at least 4′ wide x 5′ long x 8′ high.
			  b. No windows in carrel door.
			  c. Indirect incandescent white lights in ceiling and an extra lamp (gooseneck, spotlight-type).

Description of Specific Requirements — (Continued)

Area Code	Description of Space	Net Assignable Sq. Ft.	Remarks
			d. Counter across one end of booth. e. Two speakers should be separately wired so that two different program sources can be easily distinguished by the person(s) recording. f. On a hook to one side of the counter should be a headset with earphones and two microphones. The jacks for this equipment should be located in the panel on the counter. g. Under the counter on one side will be a bookshelf. h. Acoustically treated floors. i. Coat hook in each booth. j. A chair and wastebasket to be included in each booth. k. Dual-machine recording unit with electronics located on racks outside booth, but visible to occupant through acoustically treated window in rear wall. l. Warning light, signaling when user is recording, on outside of each booth and interconnected with microphone circuits. m. Complete sound proofing with sound interlocks on doors. n. Noise level from air conditioning must be kept sufficiently low to allow for professional recordings. o. Electrical conduits going from each booth and terminating at tape decks. 10. In addition to the above for all booths, one will be equipped with a short-wave receiver, one with a turntable, and two with PLATO-type equipment, for on-line authoring and editing.

J-6	Visual Teaching Equipment	450	The room will be used in the following ways: (1) for individualized use as an instructor tapes his own performances at a lectern in order to review them by immediate playback; (2) for small-group use for playback of previously produced video tapes; (3) for use as a video monitoring station for the library labs; (4) for storage of projectors to be used in the classrooms.
			This room will be divided into four areas, according to use made of it:
			1. Darkroom, approximately 5' x 8', with the following specifications:
			  a. One counter at table height on side of room.
			  b. A door with light seal.
			  c. Counter and darkroom sink with

Description of Specific Requirements — (Continued)

Area Code	Description of Space	Net Assignable Sq. Ft.	Remarks
			running water (hot and cold) at end of room.
			d. Closed wall cabinets with adjustable shelves, about 18″ above counters, for supplies.
			e. Light switch controlling both incandescent and infrared light sources.
			f. Warning light over outside door.
			g. Standard darkroom equipment.
			2. Video monitoring and editing room, approximately 15′ x 8′, having the following equipment:
			a. A special lectern with remote-control operating a video camera and slant trait video tape recorder.
			b. Video camera (vidicon).
			c. Video tape monitor.
			d. PLATO station (including individual audio record unit).
			e. One comfortable, low, lounge-type chair with table extension.
			f. Three chairs.
			The remaining two areas of the room should be made semi-separate by means of temporary partitions:
			3. Storage area for portable visual equipment, with shelves of appropriate sizes for the following equipment:
			a. Overhead projectors.
			b. Opaque projectors.
			c. 16mm sound projectors.
			d. 8mm cartridge projectors.
			e. Filmstrip projectors.
			f. 35mm slide projectors.
			g. Portable screens.
			h. Two movable rear projection units for previewing films and slides for classroom use.
			i. Several 18″ x 24″ x 3′ rolling stands (with 20′ extension cords) for use with various projectors throughout Foreign Languages Building.
			4. Instructional material preparation area.
			a. Work table.
			b. Drawing board and drawing board chair.
			c. Table for machines and enough space between for preparation of projectuals (approximately 18′ x 4′).
			d. Storage cabinets for art materials.
			e. Five tablet-arm chairs.
			f. Equipment:
			(1) Dry mount press
			(2) Contour — constat

Description of Specific Requirements — (Continued)

Area Code	Description of Space	Net Assignable Sq. Ft.	Remarks
			(3) Polaroid copy maker
			(4) A system for production of Diazochrome multicolored transparencies: a portable platen printer consisting of (1) a light box; (2) a combination drawing board, mounting board, and platen; (3) a contact printing assembly consisting of an aluminum compression tray, foam rubber compression pad, and printing glass cover; (4) a special punch; (5) a "pickle jar" developer; and (6) a special stapler.
			(5) A 35mm slide copier consisting of camera on special stand to permit enlarging, cropping, double exposure, color control, etc.
			(6) Thermofax infrared copier for carbon-base instruction materials, suitable for making ditto masters and black and white or color transparencies (table model about 2' x 2').
			(7) Dry photo copier (table model about 3' x 2').
			(8) Poster typewriter (about 2' x 2' table model) on typing table, with typist's swivel chair.
			(9) Filing cabinets for filmstrips (over all dimensions 6' x 40" x 24").
			(10) Filing cabinet for transparencies.
			(11) Filing cabinet for 35mm slides.
			(12) Light table (built-in) for 35mm previewing.
			Adequate ventilation for photographic processing; electrical outlets (two for clocks, one for refrigerators) that are hot at all times, rest of lights and outlets on a master room control current with controls by all doors. A phone should be provided (wall-mounted).
J-7	Remote Equipment Rooms (2)	360 Each 720 Total	In the remote equipment rooms will be housed the following equipment: a. A PLATO multiplex unit. b. A minimum of 16 PLATO-compatible audio program units; each program stored in these units should be capable of being audited simultaneously, at the same or at different points in the program (with one-half-second access time) by as many students as may desire to work with that program or as are being tested at available student positions.

Description of Specific Requirements — (Continued)

Area Code	Description of Space	Net Assignable Sq. Ft.	Remarks
			c. A minimum of 224 PLATO-compatible audio record units (one per student station), each unit providing two-second access to any point in a two-minute recorded student passage, with the possibility of longer student recordings (with 16-second access) for special purposes, this recording taking place while all students are listening (for recording cues) to the same program or each to a different one of the 16 available programs. d. A time-shared automatic video tape recorder with random access. e. A time-shared automatic movie projector with random access.
J-8	Program Storage (2)	180 Each 360 Total	These rooms will be used for the storage of tapes, discs, and time-shared audio programs. Ceiling-height metal shelves will be required, dimensions to be determined at a later date.
J-9	Library-type Language Laboratories (2)	1,680 Each 3,360 Total	Each laboratory is to contain 49 PLATO-type multimedia learning carrels. The precise specifications are unknown at this time and will be provided after prototype testing. The learning carrels must be capable of being connected with the campus-wide television system.

J-10	Classroom-type Language Laboratories (6)	840 Each
		5,040 Total
			Each lab will have the following:
			1. Minimum of 21 prefabricated relocatable PLATO booths, approximately 10 square feet each, which can be attached to one another and arranged in rows all facing toward the front of the room.
			2. Center aisle 3′ wide, with lateral aisles also 3′ wide.
			3. In each booth will be the following equipment:
			  a. Headset with earphones and microphone.
			  b. PLATO video monitor.
			  c. PLATO teletype input apparatus.
			4. Movable slanted shelves for mimeographed materials, etc., located on the wall to the right of the student access door.
			5. Two doors to the lab; one at the back of the room for student access, and one at the front giving access to the raised platform from the hall.
			6. Raised platform, across front of the room. On this platform will be the following:
			  a. Two electrically operated projection screens, 70″ x 70″, one located on the center front wall (squarely

Description of Specific Requirements — (Continued)

Area Code	Description of Space	Net Assignable Sq. Ft.	Remarks
			behind the overhead projector), the other located on the left front wall in such a way as to receive the image from a projector located in the center aisle. b. Two padded metal chairs and one padded metal chair with silenced rollers but no arms. c. Console, 5' x 2½', will be located on the platform at right center front (as seen from the student area). This console will contain a PLATO station (with individual audio record unit) and an automatic tape playback. d. Overhead projector on movable stand (18" x 24" x 3') will be at center front, adjacent to console. e. Console and overhead projector will have metal covers which can be locked during unscheduled hours in the lab. f. Telephone with flashing light (NOT a bell) at each console. g. Five lockable storage cabinets, 2' wide x 2½' deep x 8' high, with adjustable shelves. Three cabinets are to be located at left wall on platform and two between console and right wall. h. Entire wall behind platform is to be occupied by six sliding chalkboards, ceiling height, with 9" built-in bookshelves behind them. Each combination chalkboard-bookshelf unit is to be equipped with a lock, so each language department will have its own storage space. Each board will slide only far enough to give access to that unit's shelves. 7. Ceiling no lower than 11' for effective use of projectors in rooms twice the length of an ordinary classroom. 8. The floors of both the platform and the student area should be chosen with both aesthetic and sound absorption qualities in mind. The room is full of "live" microphones and room noises are very distracting, especially when the teacher is using the microphone at the console. 9. Twenty-one padded metal chairs, with shelves underneath for student belongings. 10. Coat racks across back of room. 11. One clock. 12. All outlets and equipment (except

Description of Specific Requirements — (Continued)

Area Code	Description of Space	Net Assignable Sq. Ft.	Remarks
			clock) for each room are to be controlled by one master switch located on the console. 13. For comments on duct system, see General Considerations. 14. Booths must be capable of being connected to the campus-wide closed-circuit TV system.
J-11	Director's Office	180	This office will contain: desk and chair, adjustable shelving standards, work table, filing cabinets, side chairs, bulletin board (4' x 6'), provisions for monitoring video and audio, provisions to hang coat(s) and hat(s), and wastebasket. In addition, there will be a PLATO station (including individual audio record unit).
J-12	Assistant Director's Office	120	This office will contain: desk and chair, adjustable shelving standards, work table, filing cabinets, side chairs, bulletin board (4' x 6'), provisions for monitoring video and audio, provisions to hang coat(s) and hat(s), and wastebasket. In addition, there will be a PLATO station (including individual audio record unit).
J-13	Secretary and Reception	240	This office area is to contain: secretary desk and chair, filing cabinet(s), four side chairs, storage wall 2' x 10' with sliding and locking doors and adjustable shelving, 4' x 6' bulletin board, dictionary on stand, provisions to hang coats and hats, electric typewriter.
J-14	Program Coordinator's Offices (2)	90 Each 180 Total	Each office is to contain: 1. Console with six tape recorder playbacks and access equipment for remote-control of desired equipment for programming purposes. 2. Counter forming "L" with console. 3. Coat hooks. 4. Provisions for monitoring video and audio. 5. PLATO station (including individual audio record unit). 6. Movable equipment is to include chair, bulletin board, and bookcase.
J-15	Staff Lounge	120	This room is to be furnished with lounge furniture, base counter with sink and storage cabinet above. This counter should be designed so that it can be closed off when not in use.

APPENDIX E

Status Sheet

Building Number		Building Name			Date		
Function	**Proposed**	**Programmed**	**Grant Application**	**Preliminary**	**Working Drawing**	**Final Invoice**
Date						
1 Classrooms						
2 Instructional Labs						
3 Instructional Gyms						
4 Office Space						
5 Library Space						
6 Auditorium, Theaters, etc. not used for instruction						
7 Gyms, Armory, etc. not used for instruction						
8 Housing Area						
9 Commons						
10 Campus Hospital and Health Facilities						
11 Building and Grounds Maintenance						
12 Research Space						
13 Lab School						
14 Athletic Association						
15 Quasi-University						
16 Inactive Space						
17 Warehouse Storage						
18 Total Net						
19 Total Gross						
20 Mechanical						
21 Circulation						
22 Custodial						
23 Construction						
24 Net/Gross						

Comments:

INDEX

Administrative units: storage space requirements, 61-62
Agriculture: instructional laboratory space requirements, 55; office space requirements, 56-58; research space requirements, 59; storage space requirements, 62
Archive and research equipment storage: definition of, 61
Armed Forces: instructional laboratory space requirements, 56; office space requirements, 56; research space requirements, 61; storage space requirements, 64
Auditoriums not for instruction: definition of, 68
Auxiliary service: definition of, 24
Building blocks: definition of, 17, 51
Building efficiency: components of, 95; definition of, 18, 94; example of, 94
Buildings and grounds. *See* Physical plant
Business office stores. *See* Purchasing stores
Circulation area: definition of, 8
Class period: definition of, 17
Classroom: calculation of space requirements, 52-53; definition of, 23, 52
Commerce: instructional laboratory space requirements, 55; office space requirements, 56; research space requirements, 59; storage space requirements, 62
Commons space: calculation of space requirements, 66; definition of, 66
Construction area: definition of, 9
Course and student-level file: definition of, 42; example of, 43
Course facility file: definition of, 42; example of, 42
Custodial area: definition of, 7

Definitions of building areas: circulation area, 8; construction area, 9; custodial area, 7; gross area, 6; interior area, 9; mechanical area, 8; net assignable area, 7
Definitions of types of facilities: archive and research equipment storage, 61; auditoriums not for instruction, 68; commons space, 66; gymnasiums not for instruction, 68; health services, 67; inactive, 68; instructional laboratories, 53; library space, 64; museums not for instruction, 68; office space, 56; physical plant space, 66; purchasing stores, 70; research space, 58
Definitions of usage of rooms by function: auxiliary service, 24; classroom, 23; field buildings, 24; laboratory, 24; library, 24; office, 23; physical plant services, 24; special laboratory, 24; university services, 24; warehouse, 24
Definitions of utilization terms: class period 17; net assignable square feet per station, 17; room period usage, 17; station utilization, 17; student station, 17; weekly student hour, 17
Education: instructional laboratory space requirements, 55; office space requirements, 56; research space requirements, 59; storage space requirements, 62
Engineering: instructional laboratory space requirements, 55; office space requirements, 56; research space requirements, 59; storage space requirements, 63
Faculty data: requirements for, 47; format for collecting, 47; calculating office requirements, 48
Field buildings: definition of, 24

Field of study: definition of, 18
Fine and Applied Arts: instructional laboratory requirements, 55; office space requirements, 56; research space requirements, 60; storage space requirements, 63
Government and Public Affairs: office space requirements, 56; research space requirements, 61; storage space requirements, 64
Graduate College: research space requirements, 60; storage space requirements, 63
Graduate students: requirements for projecting space, 45; format for collecting data, 46. *See also* Students
Gross area: definition of, 6
Gymnasiums not for instruction: definition of, 68-70
Health service: calculation of space requirements, 68; definition of, 67
Inactive space: calculation of space requirements, 68; definition of, 68
Instructional laboratories: definition of, 53; method of calculating space requirements, 53-56
Instructional laboratory space requirements: Agriculture, 55; Armed Forces, 56; Commerce, 55; Education, 55; Engineering, 55; Fine and Applied Arts, 55; Journalism, 56; Liberal Arts and Sciences, 56; Library Science, 56; Physical Education, 56
Interior area: definition of, 9
Inventory. *See* Physical facilities inventory
Journalism: instructional laboratory space requirements, 56; office space requirements, 56; research space requirements, 60; storage space requirements, 63
Laboratory space: definition of, 24. *See* Instructional laboratories. *See also* Research space or Special laboratory
Labor relations: research space requirements, 61; storage space requirements, 64
Law: classroom space requirements, 72; commons space requirements, 73; courtroom space requirements, 73; forum space requirements, 73; instructional laboratory space requirements, 72; library space requirements, 72-73; office space requirements, 72; research space requirements, 72; storage space requirements, 72

Level of student: definition of, 18; example of, 42-44
Liberal Arts and Sciences: instructional laboratory space requirements, 56; office space requirements, 56; research space requirements, 60-61; storage space requirements, 63-64
Library Science: instructional laboratory space requirements, 56; office space requirements, 56; research space requirements, 61; storage space requirements, 64
Library space: basis for calculating stack requirements, 49, 65; calculation of space requirements, 65-66; definition of, 24, 64
Lounge space. *See* Commons space
Mechanical area: definition of, 8
Museums not for instruction: definition of, 68
Net assignable area: definition of, 7
Net assignable square feet per station: definition of, 17
Net-to-gross ratio. *See* Building efficiency
Numeric method: philosophy of, 1, 51; purpose of, 51; sample calculation of, 82-83
Office: calculation of space requirements, 56-57; definition of, 23, 56
Physical Education: instructional laboratory space requirements, 56; office space requirements, 56; research space requirements, 61; storage space requirements, 64
Physical facilities inventory: definition of, 17; elements of, 20; examples of, 100-21; file maintenance procedure, 28-40; procedure for starting, 30-40; requirements of, 19; schedule numbers for, 25-26
Physical plant: calculation of space requirements, 66-67; definition of, 24, 66
Program statement: definition of, 17
Purchasing stores: calculation of space requirements, 70; definition of, 70
Recreation space. *See* Gymnasiums not for instruction
Research space: definition of, 58; method of calculating space requirements, 58-59
Research space requirements: Agriculture, 59; Armed Forces, 61; Commerce, 59; Education, 59; Engineering, 59-60; Fine and Applied Arts, 60; Government and Public Affairs, 61; Graduate Col-

lege, 60; Journalism, 60; Labor Relations, 61; Liberal Arts and Sciences, 60-61; Library Science, 61; Physical Education, 61; Social Work, 61

R.O.T.C.: uniform storage requirements, calculation of, 70. *See also* Armed Forces

Room period usage: definition of, 17

Social Work: office space requirements, 56; research space requirements, 61; storage space requirements, 64

Special laboratory: definition of, 24

Staff data: requirements for projection, 47-49

Station utilization: definition of, 17

Storage. *See* Archive and research equipment storage

Storage space standards: administrative units, 61-62; Agriculture, 62; Armed Forces, 64; Commerce, 62; Education, 62-63; Engineering, 63; Fine and Applied Arts, 63; Government and Public Affairs, 64; Graduate College, 63; Journalism, 63; Labor Relations, 64; Liberal Arts and Sciences, 63-64; Library Science, 64; Physical Education, 64; Social Work, 64

Student clock hour. *See* Weekly student hour

Student contact hour. *See* Weekly student hour

Student health service. *See* Health service

Student mix: definition of, 18; example of, 44-45

Student station: definition of, 17

Student station period of occupancy. *See* Weekly student hour

Students: advanced graduate, 18; beginning graduate, 18; full-time equivalent, 18; level of, 18; mix of, 18; lower division, 18; upper division, 18

Undergraduate students. *See* Students

University services: definition of, 24

Vending space. *See* Commons space

Veterinary Medicine: animal quarters space requirements, 75-77; classroom space requirements, 74; clinic facility requirements, 78-80; commons space requirements, 75; instructional animal quarters space requirements, 77; instructional laboratory space requirements, 74; library space requirements, 75; locker and clean-up space requirements, 75; office space requirements, 74; research animal quarters space requirements, 79-80; research laboratory space requirements, 74-75; storage space requirements, 80

Warehouse space: definition of, 24

Weekly room hours. *See* Room period usage

Weekly scheduled hours. *See* Room period usage

Weekly student hour: definition of, 17